THE CUCKOO IN JUNE

The author tells how, in 1954, he abandoned the secure life of a chartered accountant and bought a small apple farm in the Weald of Sussex. With no knowledge of fruit farming, he found himself at a loss in a strange, rural world. He tells, with many an amusing anecdote, how the farm survived drought, frost and hail and for a time prospered. The surge of Golden Delicious and the strangling power of the supermarkets nearly drove the farm to the wall, but with the help of skilled staff it still survives as a happy place.

DAVID ATKINS

THE CUCKOO IN JUNE

Tales of a Sussex Orchard

Complete and Unabridged

ULVERSCROFT
Leicester

First published in Great Britain in 1992

First Large Print Edition
published 1996

British Library CIP Data

Atkins, David, *1916* –
 The cuckoo in June: tales of a
Sussex orchard.—Large print ed.—
Ulverscroft large print series: non-fiction
1. Atkins, David, *1916*–
2. Orchards—England—East Sussex
3. Large type books
I. Title
634.1′1′092

ISBN 0–7089–3624–5

Published by
F. A. Thorpe (Publishing) Ltd.
Anstey, Leicestershire

Set by Words & Graphics Ltd.
Anstey, Leicestershire
Printed and bound in Great Britain by
T. J. Press (Padstow) Ltd., Padstow, Cornwall

This book is printed on acid-free paper

'He was but as the cuckoo is in June,
Heard, not regarded.'

Shakespeare, Henry IV

Foreword by
Sir Francis Avery Jones FRCP

Drawings by
Roger Smith

This book is dedicated to my staff, who, intelligent and sensitive to the needs of nature, work outside in all weathers and enjoy it.

They are:

Michael Hutchinson
and
Janice Goodsell
Molly Flaherty
Michael Squires
Clive Weston

Foreword
by
Sir Francis Avery Jones CBE MD FRCP
President
British Digestive Foundation (BDF)

Those who have read David Atkins' two successful books on the Burma campaign will enjoy again his racy style interspersed with valuable information. Here are the successes and tribulations, starting from scratch, achieving success but then witnessing the collapse of the apple industry. It traces the story of the apple from the planting of the orchard through all the problems of growing, harvesting and marketing, and into the consumer's home. He became one of the well known apple farmers in the country. In 1985 he and his son were awarded the prestigious Elgar Memorial Rose Bowl, then given only for valuable research work or for an outstanding orchard. The book finishes on a sad note with the rapid decline of English apple farming. Easier growing conditions in warmer climates have led to greatly increased imports; many English orchards have been 'grubbed up' with growers going out of business.

For variety, versatility and flavour the English apple has no peer and the survival of a home apple industry is vital. Help may come from an unexpected quarter. I am a retired physician long concerned with digestive diseases. I believe it is only a matter of a year or two before there will be a far greater appreciation of the vital role fruit and vegetables play in our nutrition. The national scene has been dominated by coronary heart disease and an increase in some forms of cancer. Dietary advice has concentrated on the hazards of fat of animal origin in promoting heart disease. Far too little attention has been given to the concept that there are dietary factors which provide protection against injury to blood vessels. These protective factors have been depleted by increasing factory refinement, over-processing and inappropriate domestic preparation of food, but they are found in whole grain cereals, in vegetables, in pulses and in fruit. I foresee a considerable increase in demand for vegetables and fruit.

Human life has evolved over several million years as 'Hunter-Gatherers' with a basic diet of nuts, grain, roots and fruit providing our essential vitamins and minerals. This has been augmented by irregular feasts from the successful hunt. All animal, bird and insect life has evolved with its own food environment. In Britain today we overplay the 'hunter' diet and badly underplay the 'gatherer' foods and as a result we now find ourselves near the top of the world league tables for heart disease and some cancers. It is attributed to having too much animal fat but is this true? In some Mediterranean countries we find just as much fat being consumed, but more fruit and vegetables and far less heart disease. The link could prove to be not with animal fat but with the protective factors present in fruit, vegetables and whole grain cereals. In the forties when the Ministry of Health ran a nation-wide campaign for 'protective foods' the health of the nation was remarkably good and there was no epidemic of heart diseases in younger people.

Scientists have identified factors which

protect our blood vessels against fats. To ensure their supply we should double our consumption of fresh fruit and salads and, in addition to using more whole grain cereals, increase the use of raw and cooked vegetables. All are foods in which these factors are concentrated.

Remember the old adage 'An apple a day keeps the doctor away'. The apple itself can make its own contribution. In it there is a vital amount of vitamins and trace elements, its fibre contributes towards the good functioning of the bowels, its sugar is absorbed slowly and does not worry the teeth, which indeed may benefit from the texture. The apple could again serve as the spearhead to stimulate an interest in eating more fresh foods day by day. What a major impact apples could have on the health of the nation, for all fruit growers, and for our countryside! We shall say 'An apple a day keeps your heart attack away'!

Sir Francis Avery Jones CBE MD FRCP
British Digestive Foundation
3 St. Andrew's Place Regent's Park
London NW1 4LB

Introduction

WHEN I started as a fruit farmer in Sussex in 1954 there were three thousand apple growers in England. The gossip in the Clubs was that this was a good thing to get into; half the Cabinet and also the Queen had just planted up. Now there are just eight hundred of us left and the Queen's orchards at Sandringham only survive because of the cachet of buying apples direct from her estates. In a few more years apple growing in England may have gone the way of the plough horse. Are we June Cuckoos?

This tale charts the changing pattern of failure and success in apple growing. It covers thirty five years in which the apple industry, from a low start, prospered for a time and then fell back to the edge of collapse.

It is also the story of the gradual 'greening' of an industry which, to a remarkable degree has cleaned itself up and started doing so long before the pressure groups became busy.

The events recorded are factual but some characters, particularly Funnell, are a mixture of Sussex types.

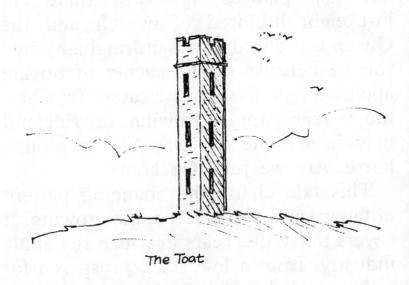

The Toat

1

The Gamble

"**Y**OU'VE done what?" said my father incredulously.

"I've resigned from Coopers."

"You've resigned from Coopers!" he repeated. "Why did you do that when you'd just become senior partner?"

"Only in Bulawayo," I replied, "and I've decided to stay in England and go apple farming."

"Apple farming!" said my father with astonishment, "did you say apple farming? But our family have always been in the professions," he paused, "and you haven't any money."

"I've got £20,000," I said, "£23,000 to be exact."

"Where did you get that?" My father, although the most mild and level-headed of men, was finding this conversation difficult to come to terms with. Why should his son, a chartered accountant,

3

wish to leave the security of a profession? "That won't be enough and I can't afford to finance you," Later he said. "I'll give you one thing though — I'll stand you the services of Basil Furneaux, He's the best soil consultant in England. He may keep you out of trouble."

Basil Furneaux and my father had worked together throughout the Second World War. They had decided where the airfields and barracks in the south of England should be placed, and in so doing had kept the best soils free for farming and feeding the nation.

Basil Furneaux was a painful blessing. As fast as I found lovely farms which I wished to buy he dismissed them. At last I came up with one near Pulborough, sixty acres for £16,000, one cottage and twenty four acres of apple trees which had been well planted by German prisoners of war in 1946. As we walked round the fields taking soil samples he noticed there was another apple farm next door.

"That's for sale too," I remarked, "but I can't afford to buy it."

He stopped and looked at the house which lay long, low and cosy beneath old elm trees. There was no smoke from the chimneys.

"No-one at home," he said, "come on, jump the ditch and we'll look."

We scrambled across and through the hedge. With his auger he took several samples.

"Badly managed trees, but quite good soil, you'll have to buy it."

"I can't afford it."

"Nonsense, you'll never have the chance again. A good house — two cottages thrown in — that makes three — and you'll have over a hundred acres of tolerable soil, forty of it planted. Buy it."

"But if I buy it, I'll have no money left in reserve."

"An apple farmer with reserves? — they all live on overdrafts. If you buy one farm you'll probably be down and out in three years; if you buy the two you may survive, and with luck and hard work you might even succeed."

★ ★ ★

The owners of the two farms were bitter enemies. They had quarrelled so frequently

5

that, in order to get away from each other, they had each put their farm on the market without telling the other.

There was no nonsense about dealing through estate agents. I dealt direct.

I went up to London to see the owner of the second farm, Tullens. He disliked his wife's friends and was selling to get her away from them. He was easy to deal with.

"I bought the farm for £14,000, the market has gone down by 10%, I want to sell — that is another £1,000 off — £11,500 and it's yours." I asked for a month's option, which he gave me.

The owner of the first farm, Toat Lodge, was extremely rich, but he seemed for the moment to be set in a pattern of disaster. He had been drilling for oil in Canada for two years, had decided it was useless, and sold the well. The next week the new owner struck oil. His wife had just left him and two world famous pictures he had bought had turned out to be fakes. He took me to lunch at Scott's.

"I can't pay £16,000," I said, "I haven't got the money."

"I'll give you a mortgage."

"I don't approve of mortgages."

"That is a very sensible attitude; how much can you afford?"

"I can afford £10,000."

"Right, I'll sell it to you."

"I need an option while I think about it."

"Get your solicitor to send me an option and I'll sign it."

"If I write out an option now, would you sign it?" I asked.

"Yes," he replied, "anything to avoid legal fees."

Anything to avoid legal fees from my solicitor

I turned over the menu and wrote:

I, Charles Smith, in exchange for 2/6, sell David Atkins a month's option from today to buy the sixty acre farm known as Toat Lodge for £10,000.

7

Immediately after lunch I telephoned my solicitor.

"Did you pay him the 2/6?" he asked.

"No".

"Give me his address and I'll send him a bank draft for 2/6 today by special messenger." By this somewhat unusual means I bought the two adjoining farms. I had no money left and I had little knowledge of fruit growing.

Toat Hill is crowned with a slim stone tower; it stands where once the Druid signal fires burnt. The farm to the south looks to the Downs and to the west faces across the water meadows of the Arun Valley to the ancient woods of Stopham. There is hardly a building in sight.

There was delay before I took over Toat Lodge as they wanted to pick the crop. Meanwhile Smith was helpful. He drove me down from London and took me round the farm with his foreman, Funnell.

Afterwards, as we were driving back to London, we stopped at a roadside garage. Smith was a man of impulse.

"I won't be long," he said. "I'm just going to buy a car for the Funnell girls."

Within five minutes he was back. "It will be delivered later in the week."

"Can the girls drive?" I asked.

"No, but they can learn. They are cut off from everyone. That tough old father will never drive them anywhere."

The car was delivered. Alfred Funnell walked round it as though it was the wooden horse of Troy. Then he drove it off and sold it the same day.

I moved in to Tullens in the summer of 1954. I had inherited a few good pictures, and some furniture. I bought everything else I needed on a rainy day at an auction sale in a large decrepit farmhouse. The furniture and crockery was all forty years old or more and now all of it has gone except for some lovely egg cups and old moustache cups. The house was large and empty. The wind blew every day, the windows were curtainless, the floors had no carpets, and I got bad hay fever. I felt I had made a terrible mistake. I now had no income.

The one bright spot was that with the house came the most motherly of daily helps, Mrs. Mills, who cooked for and looked after me. Her presence I owed to

Mrs. Mills was my gain

the sacking of her husband by a neighbour, This neighbour had been going round her large garden with Mills. All her remarks were met with a hostile silence.

"What is the matter with you, Mills?" she asked, "I never criticise your work."

"It's not the bloody silly things you say, Madam," he replied "it's the bloody silly things you think."

He had to go, and her loss of Mrs. Mills was my gain — my great gain.

The last thing Mrs. Mills did for her former employer was, she told me, to collect every pair of shoes and riding boots in the house and, with tears running down her face, clean all fifty pairs. She loved the family of five girls and was loved in return.

Each day at breakfast I got my local news from Mrs. Mills. When the Funnell girls' car arrived she told me what happened.

"That Funnell, Master David," she said, "has sold the girls' car, without a word of a by-your-leave. Sold it and pocketed the money,"

Mills had been used to working only a thirty five hour week and he now volunteered to work another half an hour daily, It was a crisis point; if I had agreed all my future staff would have worked less than the national 42 hour week (now 39 hours). Basil Furneaux had prepared me, however.

"Make sure your staff work the hours agreed by their trade union, just say that when fixing their pay." I made the point now, realising as I did so that Mills's offer was intended to put me in a false position. Unlike his wife, who had a warm and generous heart, he delighted in any mistake I made, and I made a great many.

* * *

When the Toat Lodge crop was picked, Funnell joined me. I found him to be

11

very knowledgeable; very Sussex and very silent. (Sussex folk came up the rivers from Saxony about 300 AD). Already wizened at forty five, probably by years of underfeeding in the 1930s when farm workers were paid about ten shillings a week, he didn't like people and he showed it. I made a bad start by calling him by his surname only, This school and army habit entraps many a business

Funnell did not like people and he showed it.

man turned farmer. It infuriated him and he took to not answering me. One of his daughters enlightened me.

"Please call my father Mr. Funnell."

"Call him Mr. Funnell?" I repeated with some astonishment "I can't do that."

"He calls you Mr. Atkins, doesn't he?"

"Would it be all right if I called him Alfred?"

"I'll ask him," she said.

Next morning she waited for me: "Yes, you can call him Alfred."

Among Sussex people the use of the surname by itself was, and perhaps is, regarded as an intimacy. Wives often used their husband's surnames, not their Christian names, when talking to and of them.

From the house on Tullens I had watched all the long summer as Toat Lodge went to pieces. I was due to take possession after the harvest, but from the day we signed, the spraying and the grass cutting had deteriorated. At last the handover came. The first job that Alfred did for me was to lay a coker (Sussex for a small bridge) across the ditch that lay between the two farms. Mills I had now more or less under control, but Funnell and his family were to prove a tougher job. This problem of taking over staff in farming is a very common one, one works so closely with them. The Funnells' method of insubordination was to take one hour and twenty minutes for an hour's lunch break.

"You're late back Alfred."

"Can't manage quicker, that's for sure."

"But your daughters could."

"Can't ruin me darters' stomachs."

Funnell was a slow eater

It was true he was a slow eater, I had watched the twenty minute break at 10 o'clock. They sat down promptly, but when they rose thirty-five minutes later Alfred was still chewing.

That first winter we only had one moment of comradeship, I had kept back the whole of the Tullens crop for the Christmas trade. It was only fifty boxes which were in a stable. I saw three rats run in under the door and I called Alfred; he brought his dog and we both went in with sticks. As we moved box after box the rats ran out, young and old. Our sticks fell and fell and his dog seized and shook, seized and shook. When the last rat was dead the blood had splattered up on our boots and trousers and the dog's ruff was dripping red. Forty-six rats lay dead. I had to throw away all my first crop. Since then I have had a horror of rats. Even dead they carry dangerous diseases.

That winter the pruning dragged on and on. The canker, coming after the scab let in by poor spraying, was rampant and the Funnells were, I was sure, going slow.

"Alfred, we have forty acres of Cox to complete and we're only halfway through: it's already March."

Later Alfred and I were to get on very well together. I realised his resistance to me as an ignorant newcomer taking over a farm on which he had planted, pruned and nurtured every tree, was only natural. They were his trees and until I came along he was the manager. Now he was down to foreman and taking daily orders.

"Me, I like to do a job thorough." He was working at four trees a day while I was doing eight, though not as well as he. "Perhaps the girls might fancy a bonus per tree — that would surely help," he suggested.

I had an inspiration. I brought in eight contract pruners from Kent. They did fifteen trees a day each, not good work but the light could get into the trees and the pruning log jam was broken.

★ ★ ★

After the war I had spent four years in what was then Rhodesia, now my

16

first year at Tullens was both enlivened and made difficult for me by visitors from that colony who regarded my large house as their weekend cottage. I had received great hospitality out there from many families, and now, with the casual friendliness of Africa, they descended on me.

"Hi, sweetie, Pam and I and Julian thought of coming down for a few days." The two girls were known as the 'sweetie pies'.

"Well, I'm out on Saturday evening, so - - - "

"Not to worry sweetie, we'll look after ourselves."

I set them to shop and to tractor drive, to fetch the wages, to cook and to do carpentry. They bunked down around the house on the bare floor boards in the curtainless rooms. It was amusing but not helpful to the farm. Avril ran the tractor into an apple tree and knocked it down, Pam ran into a beehive and was lucky to get away with her life, and then Julian crashed my one tractor into the barn, After this I ceased trying to make them useful and just accepted their charming presence around the house. One weekend Avril said:

"What you need, sweetie, is a dog. I'll give you one for your birthday."

"Good idea," I said "I'd like a dog."

A week later the owner of the pet shop off Berkeley Square telephoned me.

"We are delivering your white poodle tomorrow. Could you please have £120 in cash ready."

"£120 for a poodle!"

"She's a very good poodle with a long pedigree."

"I don't want a poodle. I want a mongrel."

"A mongrel!" She said in horror.

"Yes, a mongrel." She put down the telephone. I rang Avril.

"Do you usually charge up people's birthday presents to them?"

"Only to you, sweetie. You looked so lonely last weekend when I left. I'll pay you back when I get a modelling job."

"Listen Avril, can I get it into your lovely head that I have no money?"

"Well, you can always sell a field or two. You seem to have lots of spare ones."

Avril ended up as the wife of the South African delegate to the United Nations in New York. With her charming smile and love of laughter she must have helped her country enormously. As for the dog I bought a Corgi bitch, Judi, for £10. She was a jealous snappy dog, very fond of me and quite game. I used to take her shooting.

Rhodesians and South Africans, brought up in a world of cars and where there is only one railway line through each town, have great difficulty in catching the right train. The girls asked hopefully to be fetched from London —

"It's only 45 miles, sweetie" was the plaintive cry.

When they got on a train it was rarely the right one. I collected them on various occasions from Brighton, Haywards Heath and Amberley. Then I hardened my heart.

"In Brighton, are you? It will take you only an hour to get to Pulborough."

"Sweetie pie, aren't you going to fetch us — I'd fetch you!"

"No. Telephone me from the station when you get here."

19

Even now, thirty years later, whenever I employ Southern Africans, I expect and get a 50% failure rate on their catching the right train.

★ ★ ★

That next year was terrible. The neglect on both farms by the previous owners during the takeover period, now took its toll. How I wished I was back in chartered accountancy and without the burden of these farms, which were soaking up money.

How I wished I was back in chartered accountancy

Scab, black scab, that bane of all fruit growers, was rampant. It had infected every shoot and behind the scab lesions canker had run riot. The only solution was to spray with mercury, a chemical which we now never use and which was to do me no good. But I had to get a spraying machine.

Lloyd George's farm Bron-y-de was for sale. It was one Furneaux had turned down because the soil was too sandy and it was badly maintained.

"It's full of old trees neglected by old retainers who don't know how to work and would give you no loyalty. That has already been given to the Lloyd George family, particularly to his daughter Megan". She had managed most of the farm since 1945.

At the farm equipment sale there was that certain sign of bad management, sixty empty beehives and only five full ones. Bees, uncared for, quickly die out. I bought Lloyd George's sprayer and towed it by borrowed Land Rover the 25 miles from Haslemere.

It wasn't until I recently read Frances Stevenson's autobiography of her life-long love affair with Lloyd George that I realised how many dreams had gone into the making of that lovely unproductive farm, a farm which was never visited by the first Mrs. Lloyd George and where the mistress, with her long self-sacrifice and devotion, reigned. Frances, now the new Countess, owned some of the orchards and her house, Avalon. She struggled on and then sold the orchards to Chris Rhodes of whom she writes 'I had the satisfaction of seeing the orchards run by better farmers than I could ever have been'.

In fact Lloyd George had only kept the farm going by awarding himself the contract to supply the army and the NAAFI with apples. He wouldn't have got away with it nowadays.

★ ★ ★

Where we knew the old names of the fields we kept them. 'Daughteries' goes back to Norman times and was the name given to the bailiff of the high river — De haut rei. It was in that field that another neighbour, innocently I believe, enclosed half an acre of my land behind his new fence. I only discovered this when I planted it with trees and the field was smaller than I expected. After reference to the plans he gave the area back, but not before I had put a main drain in the wrong place. It still irritates me.

Two other strange names which I took over were 'Isolation' for a field surrounded by woodland and 'Long Suitors' for a big field of 14 acres, In that field we sometimes turn up winkle stone; these are rocks made of thousands of snail shells. If polished the stone is most attractive.

The name Toat is Druidic and means a look out hill. From the top of Toat we can see the next Toat 14 miles away. Before Roman times the Druids were the wise men and priests of Europe and Teut hills are found in France. Tullens has a modern origin. When Tully ran off with Helen, they set up home, unmarried, together, a matter of great scandal in the thirties. They called their house Tullens and their daughter Unity Pagan. The house was built of stone from a nearby barn and is placed in the middle of an old walled cattle enclosure. It looks south down to a stream and then on to the greensand ridge and in the distance to the South Downs. The valley must have looked the same when the Roman Legions marched down Stane Street on their way to Chichester. Indeed two of the neighbouring farms have Roman remains, one a temple to Silvanus tucked into a curve in the river and the other a villa. The only change is Toat Tower, hexagonal and slim, with slit windows in the grey stone walls, it lies behind our house and is a landmark for miles around. It was built in 1832 and is already a source of local folklore.

* * *

Day after day, throughout that hot summer, the farm staff and I, working in relays, sprayed each tree from four sides at 250 gallons an acre. In gum boots and oil skins, carrying lance guns, we plodded after the tractor. Overcome by heat and exhaustion I would lift my visor, turn to the spray drift and welcome it cool and wet on my face. At night I would wipe the mercury grey off my lips.

It cleared the scab; after each spray

the fungus spores were washed out. The orchards which had stood on the brink of disaster were pulled back. The scab lesions were clean and the canker spores could not sporulate. The mercury however gave me gout. It took twenty years to clear it out of my system. The doctors did not agree, but I still believe that is what caused it.

The autumn came. 'Season of mists and mellow fruitfulness'. The Rhodesians migrated back to their sunny country, and I was left to my large bare house, and my first full harvest. It was two thousand 30 lb boxes of the best Cox's apples I have ever seen anywhere. A flush of colour was crowned by a slight russet. I have never picked anything so uniformly beautiful since. My apples were welcomed in the markets with open arms, but of course 2,000 boxes at an average of £1 per box, less charges and transport, was about £1,500, while with Mills and Funnell and the latter's two daughters, my wages bill alone was well over £20 a week. Then there were the pickers, so my harvest only paid the wages. Wages on a fruit farm tend year after year to equal about 40% of the total cost of the farm. I had made a loss of nearly £2,000.

My loss in the first year got me three tax assessments. These arrived together in one envelope: 1954/5 (part year) nil; 1955/6 (first full year) nil; 1956/7 (previous year) nil. As I had no income I also applied for and got exemption from paying any National Insurance stamps.

With none of my staff taxable, wages took me twenty minutes a week, but now I had an overdraft. I had sold my last shares to buy a grey Ferguson tractor and a trailer and for the next season I bought an automatic sprayer. The great burden of spraying by lance was off my back.

With some time to think and breathe I began again to see the countryside. From the top of Long Suitors field, one looked over the Arun Valley which lay peaceful and studded with oak and ash trees, across the flood plain of the water meadows up to Stopham Woods owned by the same family for one thousand years. There among the chestnut coppices the short wild daffodil flourished through April to be followed by the blaze of the bluebells. The cuckoo came on time from Africa and called as it did in Chaucer's day.

"When the sweet showers of April
Have pierced the drought of March
Birds are making melodies."

I watched the apple trees changing day by day, the swelling buds turning to pink and then to bloom; the maiden wood leaping into growth and then pausing while the tree made next year's flower buds. It was all new to me.

Another crop came round and I sold £7,000 worth of apples.

"Seven thousand pounds of apples!" my father said, "at 1/- a pound that's £350, you'll have to pack it in soon."

He was amazed when I pointed out it was £7,000 sterling. My costs that year were about £6,000.

My house was still without carpets or curtains. The big rooms with my grandfather's furniture and pictures looked incongruous. But I gave some good parties, drink was cheap compared with sprays and I had been brought up in the New Forest by hospitable great aunts.

I was fortunate to meet a young doctor, only nine years younger than me, and with a happy sigh I settled down.

We were married in March 1956 and the first question Paula wanted to know was how much was our income.

"Nothing until September. Run up bills everywhere," I said, and so we did. The local tradesmen were helpful, Somehow they knew I had no mortgage.

Meanwhile Paula too had to endure the curtainless windows, the massive central heating that didn't work, the wind whistling under the doors and through the lead paned windows.

My old friends David and Didi Archer came to dinner. As he ate his soup some plaster fell into it from the ceiling. He put down his spoon.

"David," he said, "you've got to give Paula some curtains and repair some rooms in your house. This is the coldest house I have ever been in. Forget the tractors and the farm, spend some money on comfort."

And so we did, but not very much.

To Paula, used to a doctor's household, for her father too was a doctor, the way money vanishes on a farm was and still is a trial.

Paula had had little welcome from the Funnell family. Alfred, when he learned Paula and her father were doctors, held his tongue, but when I later introduced him to Paula's brother Ross, recently qualified, he could contain himself no longer. He looked at Ross in silence for a few moments.

As he ate his soup some plaster fell into it.

"Me, I doon hold with doctors," he said at last, "tidy lot of doctors there be aroun the farm nowadays".

"Yes, we're lucky."

"Do a power of harm, do doctors," said Alfred and ignoring Ross went on pruning.

I could never get Alfred into a pension scheme as when he saw a doctor his blood pressure went sky high within seconds. Our doctor, to get his blood pressure, crept up on him once in the orchard but Alfred turned and ran.

★ ★ ★

Before buying Tullens I had spent six months as a paying pupil with David and Didi Archer on their apple farm near Petersfield. There I had learnt the rudiments of picking, pruning and grading. They had planted apples in new ground. Seven years later the trees were only just beginning to crop and they were in terrible financial straits. The only thing on the farm that paid its way was me.

My dear Mrs. Mills had now gone. Mills and Alfred had been at daggers drawn so it was a relief, Now I had a vacant cottage which we filled with a charming and hard up retired army family. His county regiment gave him constant support when he became ill. His pension had never been increased since he retired as a major in 1936. I think he got £200 a year and each summer he went up to London to march with other old officers in a dwindling band of protestors. "We'll all be dead" he said to me "before they raise our pensions," Nowadays, when the Services in retirement receive good pensions, I remember him and others who fought in the First World War.

In the other lodge cottage we had a family of rogues. The father was the best pruner I have ever had and even Alfred had to admire his expertise.

"I seen him on ladder," he said, "lean right over on one leg, hook branch, pull it back and cut it, and surely it be proper cut in right place. He may be a chowse but he be no botcher."

His wife worked in the house and was no help to Paula as food and cleaning materials vanished away. The old grandmother was dirty, energetic and foul-mouthed. She worked fast and furiously but had to be kept away from everyone else for she was a great quarreller. One of the boys was in a Borstal.

At last I sacked him and his family. He flitted without letting the son know where he had gone. Nowadays one would never be able to get rid of a man like that. The new system is a sad drag on both farmer and good staff.

I replaced him with a great lumbering good-tempered ex-policeman, with a bitter nagging wife.

"She be a chatternag," said Alfred.

The new man had a tidy mind, and he loved cutting off branches with a saw, The trees looked skimmed when he had pruned them. To Paula's relief within a few months I sacked them both; he would never learn to prune. You can't grow good apples unless you have branches on which to hang them. Each fruiting branch should be about two feet from its neighbour beside it and three feet clear of any branch above or below.

Then in 1960 we got, oh joy and pleasure, an intelligent man, still with us thirty years later, and his helpful, quick-witted wife. Alan was a man who, if he had gone to University, would have got a good degree in Mathematics. He was so slight and small that he invented ways of cutting down manual work. If it could be moved by roller conveyor or on wheels he would never carry a box.

For the crop the year before he came I had myself carried every one of the 7,000 boxes up to the grader, from the grader to its appropriate quality stack and then from this stack onto a lorry. 7,000 boxes are only a hundred tons, but each box had been moved four times — 400 tons. Now, ahead of our time, we put everything on pallets and bought two pallet trucks.

★ ★ ★

Meanwhile we were having dog trouble. Judi, my corgi, disapproved of Paula's arrival and even more of our first baby. Then Paula went off to buy a dog of her own.

"Do get something small and young," I said, "preferably with short hair. We don't want dog hairs all over the place".

She found a dog who was causing trouble on a main road and was being given away free. He was an unusual Scottish long haired collie-cross, very beautiful and very unruly. To the amazement of the couple who gave him away, he got into the car with Paula, put his paw on her lap and left without a backward glance. I looked at him sourly.

"That's not a small short haired puppy".

"He's my dog," replied Paula, "and he loves me, while Judi hates me".

Judi went into a sulk followed by a phantom pregnancy. She snarled whenever Paula, our son Richard or Rusty, the collie, came into the room. I gave her away and she too went happily without a backward glance at me.

Rusty and I fought all summer for domination, Slowly he learned discipline and would come when called. In the end we loved each other deeply.

Alfred's dog, Sam, took one look at Rusty and pinned him by the throat. I rescued him. Then Sam took to coming into our house and peeing in the corridor and in my office. I asked Alfred to keep him at home.

"Aah, I mun have me dog with me, company he be."

"But he's peeing in the house", I said.

"You look after yourn," Alfred said, "and I'll see to mine."

Each time Sam came in Rusty fought him and each time was severely mauled. At last Paula, heavily pregnant, caught Sam killing Rusty in the kitchen. She hit him with the broom handle and kept it up until he released Rusty and slunk away. We never saw him near the house again.

'Aah, I mun have me dog with me, company he be'

2

The Struggle to Survive

DAVID ARCHER'S efforts were a warning to me. He had built pig sties and the price of pork had collapsed. He had bought sheep and had run into trouble with foot rot. Then their large and lovely house let them down. Built all of wood, it was found to have no damp course. They had to lift it in its entirety on car jacks and insert a new layer. Their house was full of sun, laughter and financial squalls. When there I had paid my £15 a week and on getting it David would go off to buy two bottles of whisky, one of which was gone the same evening.

David was a good grower who, after taking a great deal of advice, had bought the wrong farm. In order to be out of the frost he was 400 feet up, but no expert had foreseen that he was in a wind tunnel and the lovely fruit never made the proper size. He was always hard up and kept coming to me for advice.

"What shall I do, David? The bank won't extend my overdraft."

"Take the children away from boarding school, sell the horses and get a smaller house."

"Yes" he said. "I'll do just that."

He didn't do anything of the kind. The children and the horses soaked up all available cash and year by year he had to sell off bits of his land to keep going. On each sale he put a clause in the contract giving him the right to buy back at the sale price plus 8% compound interest. I said it was ridiculous, but the farmers happily signed. Then suddenly in two years farm land went up from £200 per acre to £2,000. He bought all the land back and resold it to the farmers at the new price. He was solvent again.

He had not long to enjoy it before he was struck by tuberculosis. He had to have one lung out and while he was in hospital Didi ran the farm with great energy and blind eyes. I went over regularly.

"I don't know what all the fuss is

about", Didi said, "the farm is quite easy to run."

"Didi, I've checked your spraying — perhaps you've put on too much sulphur. The rosette leaves for some buds are looking shrivelled."

Actually she had put on ten times the rate and that orchard did not crop.

Picking came and she rang me up when I was at my busiest. I went over with extra picking buckets. She had forty boys and girls from Bedales working there.

"Come on", she cried, "we must finish

The apples rattled in the buckets and were dropped heavily into the boxes.

this orchard today".

The apples rattled in the buckets and were dropped heavily into the boxes.

"Didi", I expostulated, "don't you think some of them are bruising?"

"Perhaps they are," and she shouted. "Don't bruise, but don't slow down. Careful and quick, that's the ticket, on — on".

Poor David, when the apples were graded 60% were bruised.

He and another fruit grower, Phillip House, formed "The Royal Naval Apple Growers Association". It had four members and I was in on an honorary basis. Every six months we dined at a pub and drank pink gins.

Brian Marston, nearby, was into machinery which he could not resist buying at sales. When spraying young apple trees he drove a thundering tractor which towed a large trailer on which was a tank and a great diesel pump. Behind this lot trailed a long thin pipe and at the far end was a small New Zealand girl with a lance. Brian on his own could have done the whole field with two knapsacks. It was a useful lesson.

When Brian had picked his small crop of two hundred boxes he stood them in a corner of David Archer's packhouse.

"I'll catch the Christmas rise," he said, looking wisely round his big nose at me.

Four weeks later he graded his apples again to get out the rotten ones. There were then 182 boxes. Four weeks later he graded his apples again and then there were 164 boxes. There was no Christmas rise and after the third grading he sold 142 boxes of rather shrivelled apples at a low price. Another lesson.

To add to his self inflicted problems he lived a hundred feet up a hill in two wooden huts built by his father for his two mistresses. These were only accessible by a steep footpath. At least his creditors, who were many, could not bother to climb the hill to find him.

Later, when Lloyd George's old farm was split up, he bought, largely on overdraft, the cold store complex. There he made poor quality cider. Inevitably he drifted into bankruptcy and the cold stores and shop were snapped up by Chris Rhodes who made them a success.

At Tullens my apple farming neighbour employed only girls. He drank hugely, dealt only in cash and was well known locally as he had announced that anyone delivering him home from a pub would be paid £5 next day (worth £100 today). He always kept his promise and was delivered home legless two or three times a week. His downfall came when the tax authorities caught up with him and he sold up in order to pay his enormous fine. Another lesson.

The apple growing world in those days seemed to be full of eccentrics. Hugh Quigley, who wrote "New Forest Orchard", lived in another wooden house near Romsey. He was renowned for spraying his orchards with liquid soap, of which he had bought up great barrels of army surplus. It kept the trees free of scab. I went to visit him. As we walked around the orchard we came across five pretty young girls in shorts. They were armed with swap hooks and were bending over trimming round the trees.

"Couldn't you get most of that done

with an Allen Scythe?" I asked.

"Is an Allen Scythe as beautiful as those smooth young legs disappearing into shorts?" he replied. I looked again and agreed it was a beautiful sight.

I had another neighbour who would never employ a man. Captain Masters left committee meetings promptly at 4 p.m., in order to take his girls home. So as to make work easy for them he only used 20 lb boxes. He was however a skilled and successful grower, producing apples of remarkable flavour. He would never put them in a cold store but kept them cool with a mist of water drawn through them by great fans.

The choice of which size box to use was a vital one. For thirty years the industry, after deserting the round cane basket, had used returnable 40 lb bushel boxes. Filled, these weighed over 52 lbs. They were owned by the wholesalers and the accounting for their movements from grower to market, on to retailers and back was expensive. Peter Wheldon in Suffolk was leading a revolution in apple marketing. The non-returnable 30 lb wooden box weighed only 34 lbs when full and any woman could handle it. The market wholesalers, in order to encourage its use, charged 7½% commission instead of the traditional 10%. This advantage was however to last only a few years. I decided to follow Peter Wheldon and use the 30 lb box, This meant that each year by early September I had to have many thousands of boxes ready on the farm.

It is remarkable how all farmers and growers are prepared to share their knowledge and lend their machines. This does not happen in the business world but in farming we walk each others' farms and freely share all knowledge and ideas. This is why farming is the most efficient industry in Britain.

★ ★ ★

When I bought Tullens a resident tramp came with it. He lived rough in an eight acre wood. The only signs one saw of him were a wisp of smoke from a tiny fire and a wigwam of sticks covered with rags. At first I tried to track him down, but he slipped away like a shadow. Once I destroyed his

to make life easy for them
he only used 20lb boxes

wigwam and looking up saw through the brushwood a reproachful eye thirty yards away.

"Hey," I called. "I don't want you in this wood."

"S'my wood," he gurgled. "S'my wood."

"No, it's mine. It really is mine."

"S'my wood."

After several efforts I gave up and

let him stay. He had some relations in Guildford and sometimes Alfred would say:

"Tramp's gone."

"Oh, where?"

"Doan rightly know — happen it's Guildford."

Twice I passed him on the way back from there. Clean, well fed and in better clothes he was hurrying home to my wood. I offered him a lift but he walked on without lifting his head. Then one year he vanished. Are his bones still there in that wood?

It's a strange wood. It was occupied by Canadian troops during the war. It is dotted with old fireplaces and soakage pits. The oaks were full of nails hammered in for clothes lines and shaving mirrors. We found a live grenade there and once Alan's daughter found a gold sovereign.

The Canadians went to Dieppe from there but few came back. They died on that steep shingle beach, enfiladed from both sides by German machine guns and under the blank eyes of the windows of the empty hotels. Was it Mountbatten's fault? If I was a Canadian mother I would feel bitter.

★ ★ ★

My annual inspection by Basil Furneaux was normally a pleasure. He never minced his words, and his instructions were clear and concise. For four years or so he had little but praise for me and then one year he was critical.

"Your trees must be thinned out. I told you so last year."

"Can't we cut them back?"

"That way lies disaster. They must have space and air to breathe and grow. You can't hold in any living thing. If it's crowded it will revenge itself on you by not giving you the crops you need."

We went back to lunch. As Paula put the soup down in front of him she asked with confidence:

"Everything as good as usual, Basil?"

"No," said Basil. "I'm afraid I must withdraw David's licence to grow Cox."

"Good heavens, what has gone wrong?" Basil's words were never taken lightly.

"When trees meet across an alley, the

trees on the diagonal must go. David has been greedy and kept them."

I took the lesson to heart. After the harvest that year Funnell and I started the slow process of choosing which trees to pull out.

"We maun stub that gurt one", he would say.

This, after four years, would result in each orchard having half their trees out, reducing them from 18 ft square and 134 trees to the acre to 25 ft square and 67 trees to the acre. The new rows ran on the cater (diagonal). This is a method of growing which is out of fashion now but may well come back. Growing methods, like women's fashions, go in cycles.

Basil gave me my fertiliser programme. On young trees he advised a natural hoof and horn mixture. He was not a great user of bagged fertilisers.

"Grass," he said, "keeps up soil fertility and organic material. Worms love it. If you have to use nitrogen put it on the trees through the grass. Your soil is most unusual in the way it locks in the phosphate — give it a little each year so that the trees will, in effect, lick the plate clean, No one knows what it does to trees but use it". Twenty years after his death they found that phosphate strengthens the cell walls in apples and helps storage. The apple makes all its cells between bloom and the end of June. The warmer the weather in June, the more cells are made. After that it is a matter of warmth and water to swell the cells.

Basil was producing a series of educational television films. He asked me to appear with him on the one on 'Clay Soils', It involved fifteen minutes on the farm and fifteen minutes live discussion. It was dubbed with our voices. On one occasion I am shown bending down over a small stunted tree.

"This great tree has become scion rooted and is out of control while" — I turn to a great tall tree which towered above me — "while this stunted one has suffered from wet feet and has never been able to grow".

The film must have confused many a child. Before the take of the interview I was handed a contract which for £18 passed over all my rights.

"This is educational work and we have a very small budget." said the producer.

Afterwards we had lunch with the TV staff. I sat next to the treasurer.

"I have so much money to spend on this programme," he confided, "I can't use it all up."

That series was shown dozens of times all over the world and I had sold all my rights for £18.

The trees at Tullens were 'delayed open centre', that is they went up with a centre leader and two tiers of branches before opening up. This contrasted with those at Toat Lodge, which were 'open centre': that is each tree had five or six main branches coming out at about 45° like a wine glass. Under Basil's tutelage I converted the delayed open centres where possible into open centre.

★ ★ ★

Cultivated apples originated somewhere in the area from the southern shores of the Black Sea down to the valleys of the Euphrates and the Tigris which was then known as the Fertile Crescent.

It is not known when man discovered the principles of grafting but it certainly goes back for four thousand years. There were orchards in Egypt in 1250 BC and the grafting of olive trees is mentioned in the Bible in Romans 11.

An apple tree grown from seed will be different from the apple tree from which it comes. Although it may have the characteristics of its mother and also of its pollinator tree, each seed will be a unique child of the union. Back in prehistory someone invented vegetative grafting; by this means a piece of wood taken from the mother tree will grow on another root but will hold all the characteristics of its mother. There are thousands of root stocks available throughout the world but if you take a slice of a Cox and graft it on to any of these you will get a Cox. On the other hand, however many Cox seeds you plant you will never get a Cox tree.

One of the strange results of this has been that throughout the whole of Europe and the Middle East there are relatively few types of apple cultivated, say perhaps nine hundred. This is because for

Back in prehistory someone invented vegetative grafting

thousands of years people have been able to get grafted trees, and have discarded the bad varieties.

In America, because the grafted trees could not survive the long voyage by sail, the early trees were all from seeds. The settlers took quantities of apples with them for the voyage and saved many seeds of these for planting. As a result in the first days of American history there may have been some hundred thousand different varieties of apple trees, all of which were unique. The number of trees became even greater because of Johnnie

Appleseed who walked across America planting seeds, each one of which created a different variety. The astonishing thing is that out of this vast number of trees America has been able to find so few good varieties. The majority of apple trees in use in the world today are from Europe. This is because selection here has taken place over thousands of years.

In Roman times the temperature in England was higher than it is now and the Romans brought with them apples and vines. In the Dark Ages it was colder, but it became warmer again at the time of the Norman Conquest. In 1400 another cold spell swept over Europe. Just before this period it is known that the pearmain and costard apples were in general use.

England is on the climatic edge of the area in which dessert apples can be grown. Our climate accounts for the good flavour of our best dessert apples which in the cool weather mature more slowly than foreign apples and have therefore a better texture.

The Cox unfortunately is a very difficult apple to grow. It is like a fragile

The Cox is like a fragile English girl

English girl who can only be pollinated with tender loving care, a warm bed and gentle handling. The French Golden Delicious is like a peasant girl who can be pollinated in a snow storm standing up against a barn. To survive, growers in England have to be more skilled than growers in France, South Africa, New Zealand or America. There the climate thrusts the trees into bearing at up to two thousand bushels an acre or even higher. The average crop of Cox in England is four hundred bushels. Even in Holland they have colder winters and warmer springs than in England. Both of these help trees to set fruit. If one has a warm February and March in England it weakens the buds and then at the end of April, when a few warm days are really needed, with an awful inevitability comes the 'blackthorn winter', a fortnight of bitter east winds which often ruin the blossom and thins the set of apples.

* * *

Every businessman turned farmer tries to use all his land and so it was with me. I had two large fields, flat and square but unsuitable for apples as they were too low. I tried wheat, very easy because it was all done by contractors. I soon ran into trouble. With only sixteen acres I had no clout to get priority of service. I made the arrangements.

"Of course I'll do your job — a pleasure — easily fit it in."

When the soil was ready it was different.

"The seed drill has jammed and I have another sixty acres I maun do before I can reach you."

So we planted late. Harvest time came round. The corn was ripe, but it had been raining. I rang up.

"I can't be everyplace at once. Look at the bloody weather we've had. I be working dawn to dusk when it be dry."

For two years running we harvested 12 cwt an acre, One ton per acre in those days was break even point; there are 20 cwts per ton.

"That be a melancholy fine crop," said Alfred.

Everyone tries pigs. Off I went to market taking Alfred with me to advise. We were going to get seven sows and turn them loose in the bluebell dell. We bought them, loaded them and trundled them home. I opened the back ramp; out rolled one large dead pig. Dead pigs are awfully heavy. The others rampaged about the dell making it look like Flanders in 1916.

I had a romantic idea about pigs, probably engendered by reading the Blandings Castle books. However I was no Lord Emsworth and I could not love them. They seemed to have too much intelligence and little affection. They caused two accidents. Horses hate pigs and my son Richard riding his new pony 'Rainy Day' was run away with and badly thrown.

Then our neighbour was riding through

the orchard when her horse, suddenly seeing the pigs, bolted through the apple trees. A branch ripped deep into the animal's nostrils and the blood spattered back over the rider. Phyllis Anne arrived at our house very shaken and with blood all over her and her horse. The first words from her generous heart were: —

"Oh David, I'm so sorry. I've knocked off a lot of your apples."

So the pigs went and the geese came. A trial batch of twelve goslings were unloaded carefully into their pen. I went to get their food. When I got back three minutes later there were only eleven, Paula and I looked everywhere; in the hutch, behind the hutch, under the straw — still only eleven. We couldn't believe it and looked again and again. It must have been a hawk.

As the goslings grew two died for no apparent reason. We moved the remaining nine into our walled garden, where they made a horrid slimy mess. We then built a large run near the kitchen garden and installed them there. They gobbled food and grew and grew and soon it was nearly Christmas. I had no idea then that foxes could open gates but this one could. Nine corpses waited for us one morning. A fox kills not only for food but for pleasure.

I had no idea that foxes could open gates but this one could.

We turned to cattle. I bought ten store cattle in the spring. They were small and weedy and cost about £20 each. They had the run of sixteen acres of excellent grass. They thrived and looked happy. I got into the habit of leaning on the gate, like a proper farmer, and enjoyed looking at them. Alfred said.

"Stand still and watch 'em. When they rises, and do stretch they be feeling well."

Is this true? I have no idea. In the autumn we took them to market and sold ten really fit animals for £20 each. Store cattle are expensive in the spring and cheap in the autumn; nobody had told me the old Sussex saying, "When the cuckoo comes to thorn, sell your cows and buy your corn".

Meanwhile around the house moles were troubling us on our lawns and I asked Alfred for advice.

"All moles," he said, "do come up to have a look around like once a day, this be between 4.15 and 4.30. Stand right over the heap they be working and bash them when they put their heads out, normally about 4.20 it be."

Did I really believe him and stand by a molehill with a spade? Yes I did. No moles came out.

"Alfred," I said, "no moles surfaced between 4.15 and 4.30."

"Ah," he replied, "that be because of summer time. Come summer time it be between 5 and 5.30." He almost smiled.

So perhaps he did have a sense of humour.

All moles do come up between 4·15 and 4:30

What's the time?

The apple grower's year consists of pruning from late November to early April. In late April or early May comes the blossom. From May to the middle of September the apples grow to be picked later in September and early October. Then in November there is a brief respite when the orchards are tidied up, the broken boxes burned, the grass cut, the soil samples taken and any sick trees pulled out. The march of the seasons waits for no man. This is a fact that only farmers and sailors understand.

That year one of my orchards was

struck by the bootlace fungus, It is a frightening disease. Get one tree with it and from there the fingers of the fungus will race out in long thin bootlaces until it finds the next tree and kills it. I believe that the fingers have some strange ability to know in which direction to go. The bootlaces never go past the tree but aim straight at it. Death comes to the next tree and to the next tree and to the next tree. Where will it stop? Oddly enough it does stop; no attack I have ever had has killed more than ten trees.

When I first planted trees it seemed to me a simple matter. With Mills to help me and a long tape measure I marked out a two-acre square and thrust in the canes at 18′ square. Up and down and across they marched in straight lines but on the diagonal they looked a mess.

"They look like horses legs!" said Mills. "That's no proper job. We best do it again."

In defiance of his criticism I planted the trees but that field was to irritate me for fifteen years until I pulled them out. I had learnt my lesson however and next time I consulted Alfred.

"You mun throw a 3 4 5," he said. I puzzled over it.

"A 3 4 5?" I asked.

"Yes," said Alfred. "Me dad tells me when I was nobut a lad to get a right angle you throw a 3 4 5." Enlightenment came to me. The square on the hypotenuse.

"You mean use the square on the hypotenuse."

"Never heard tell of that." said Alfred.

Of course that is what he was using. Three multiplied by three equals nine, four multiplied by four equals sixteen, add them together and you get twenty five, which is five multiplied by five. All we needed to do was to throw a triangle with one side of sixty feet, one side of eighty feet and one side of one hundred feet. That gave a right angle and one then extended the sixty and eighty feet lines. After that throw another triangle at the other end of the field and everything should meet up and you have a great rectangle. To get an accurate lay out on a ten acre field it takes three men almost a day: at the end the final pegs must not be more than three inches out in two hundred yards. If they are you will get "horses' legs". If you are accurate, the lines of trees will march down every row and down every diagonal in perfect symmetry. Since my first failure every field I have planted I have used the square on the hypotenuse, I learned also that metal tapes expand in the heat and cloth ones don't. All tapes used must be made of the same material on a hot day.

★ ★ ★

My father rarely came down to see us. He had remarried; she was an old girlfriend of his youth, and they lived in a flat close to Harrods from where they bought all their groceries at ridiculous prices. Their idea of comfort did not include staying in a big cold house with central heating that did not work. Occasionally they came for lunch.

"I never expected to see you live through the war," my father said. "All my contemporaries were killed in the first one. My memory of the late thirties is the horror with which your mother and I watched war approaching."

"I knew it was coming but did you?"

"Yes, but we pretended to ourselves it could not happen again. We were certain that if it did you and your brother would be killed in the trenches."

I wish I had seen more of my father in his last years.

After lunch we toured the farm and he asked about the water supply. This came from a 250 foot deep borehole. There was a big diesel pump which was extremely difficult to start. My Father took one look at the set up and said:

"You'd better get the water analysed."

Having put in the water supply for Colombo and later on for Calcutta, he was very water conscious. I protested.

"It's 250 foot deep. Surely it is bound to be pure; an analysis will cost money."

"Water's important. I'll pay for it." he replied.

So I had the water tested. The report came back 'Unfit to drink or spray on fruit trees'. Further enquiry revealed that the area of Toat was notorious in medical circles for goitre. The daughter of the family who had lived in my house during the war had had a slight case of it, as had others in the neighbourhood.

I got quotations to run a three quarter inch pipe up to the house. Two firms quoted, one to dig the trench by machine and the other by hand labour. It would be five hundred yards long, and I queried the ability of two men to dig the trench such a distance.

"Easy as anything," they replied. "Our two men can out-dig any machine at two foot six depth."

I regret to say that I chose the firm that had the machine. At the same time I put in water to the two cottages at the gate. This left my third cottage, Toat Lodge, unsupplied with mains water. They relied on a well, the water of which I also had analysed. That report started:

'This water is severely polluted.' It

then went on to detail the various horrid things which flourished there. That well also holds a gold watch. The former owner had told me that his small boy had dropped it down to see how deep the well was. What else is down there? That well is very old.

It was far too expensive to get water to the third cottage by normal means, so I bought 500 yards of quarter inch piping, which I laid along the hedges and under the bridge into the cottage. It worked perfectly well except in frosty weather when they had to use the well.

The system lasted them some six years and was a constant pleasure to Mrs. Funnell, who had brought up her large family without running water. The three comforts which change life are running cold water, running hot water and a flush lavatory. The benison of hot water has only come to farm cottages since 1950.

My clash with the Funnells was still continuing. It is easy enough in the army to keep discipline. You have the full power of rank and regulations behind you. If eighty per cent of your workforce come from one family it is not so easy.

Funnell, although a knowledgeable man and a good worker, was very untidy. Here my war training came into its own. I drove round the farm on a tractor and trailer with Funnell and together we tidied up the branches, oil tins and rotten stakes which had been accumulating there for fifteen years. Anything that stops the quick sweep of a grass cutter round a corner costs money. We hired a chain saw and cut up and carted away the fallen trees that were too big to be handled.

Without saying anything, my disapproval of his remarkable untidiness put me one up on him.

We then turned to the machinery which was lying round the farm. I would stop in front of some derelict looking object. "What is that, Alfred?"

"It be a ridger, valuable that be."

"When did you last use it?"

"Not so long ago. Maybe eight years."

"Cart it up to the main barn and we'll sell it."

His eldest daughter, Mary, was very intelligent, and when she wasn't feeling oppressed by me as a member of the capitalist classes, was a hard worker, I put her in charge of the grading, I had bought a second hand weight grader. The apples are put onto a cup by hand and as each cup reaches the right weight it is tripped and spills the apple into the proper bin for packing. It is a very slow and noisy process but used to be the one all growers used. I noticed that Mary began driving the graders hard. I came back one day from London and she said to me:

"They are a useless lot and I'm ashamed to be in charge of them."

"Look Mary," I said, "they're all we've got at the moment and all are well-intentioned. Just try and jolly them along a bit. You are ticking them off too much."

She took my advice and the grading improved considerably. I was interested to hear the other day that she now has a very senior job in London.

The next year when Alan came not merely did we palletise the movement of fruit but also I got rid of the grader. I sold it on to a friend of mine who had a passionate interest in machinery, which is a recipe for disaster for any farmer. It is excellent if a farmer can repair things but if his heart is in mechanics and not in the farm he will keep machines that would have been better consigned to the scrap heap.

The Royal Navy Apple Growers Association

3

Turkeys, Hail and Drought

IN my search for a second string to my bow I now thought of turkeys. I had some barn space free and I bought three hundred poults. They are attractive little things early on and were quite astonishingly satisfactory to feed. For every pound of food we gave them, at the beginning they put on half a pound.

Then the trouble started. As they grew bigger they developed the habit of feather pecking; there is something most unpleasant about bald and sore turkeys: they look like vultures. To stop this, the tip of each bird's beak had to be clipped off. This was a horrid job. The turkeys then developed a desire to commit suicide. Any undue noise or movement and they piled up in one corner, standing on each other's backs with the result that the bottom ones were crushed or suffocated to death.

The foxes did not help. They are quite extraordinarily cunning. They can open catches, shake wire netting until it's loose, and can squeeze through an opening which looks only big enough for a small cat. Alfred was used to them.

"Old Muster Reynolds (never Reynard) be sitting there all day a-watching us. Noting time of feed and time of lock up."

"Where do you think they are?"

"Watching us from woods one day, from that there field next. They means to get this lot."

He brought up a heavy old chain and draped it about. Each day he kicked it into a new pattern.

"That'll set ole Reynolds thinking. They'se won't cross that chain in no hurry."

Meanwhile the turkeys started eating straw which stuck in their crop. While I held them, Paula would operate with a razor blade. She would pull out the straw and sew them up again. They made no fuss and seemed to feel no pain: they healed quickly.

Now the turkeys were growing fast,

great scrawny thin birds, putting on weight, but not plump. There were few frozen turkeys in those days and every farmer seemed that year to be growing for the Christmas market, The previous year turkeys sold for about £5 each, of which £2 was profit, so now they had been overdone.

They were not far from ready when the fox struck. I swear it climbed up and stood with two paws on a pole, held onto the wire with a third paw and pulled open a big gap with its fourth paw.

They were not far from ready when the fox struck

The turkeys had piled out of the gap and we woke up early one morning, to find them loose in our shrubbery. We slowly shepherded them back, all that were left of them. Mutilated turkeys lay around us, killed for fun by the fox.

At last we came to Christmas and the killing, the plucking and the pulling out of the turkey sinews. Tim Meadows, a remarkably able and amusing countryman, helped me. He plucked three to Alfred's two and my one. Turkey plucking is a great time for stories.

Tim had done everything. He had been a male model, had run his own drainage business, had repaired barns, had been made love to by girl artists. The stories rolled out.

We finished and I took the turkeys to Petersfield market; only a few sold; to Guildford market; only a few sold; to Pulborough market; only a few sold. So I took the rest up to Leadenhall market in London where a last minute shortage occurred and they all sold well, but we made little profit.

The next in-thing in our neighbourhood was broiler chickens. Anthony Fisher, who had been at preparatory school with me, had brought the idea back from America. He had set up a processing plant at Buxted and several of my friends started up small chicken factories. Anthony supplied all the knowhow. The profits at first were startling and, in the way farmers always do, they rushed in and doubled their production. Buxted chickens became popular and while the business was still expanding, Anthony, having made sure his suppliers had sound contracts, sold up and made a million or so.

Anthony continued to make money and used it for setting up an economic research organisation which was highly regarded by Mrs. Thatcher. He died two years ago just after being knighted by her.

Anthony only lost money on one thing: he tried to do with turtles what he had done with chickens, but they put on weight too slowly and ate too much.

Dick Dutton-Forshaw, near me, tried the same system with rabbits. He ordered 400 does. When he and Tim Meadows had erected the cages, the rabbits arrived. They settled down, ate well, put on weight and appeared ready for breeding. Four special bucks were brought down.

"Put them each in a cage," he was told, "and when they have done, move them on."

Dick started at one end and Tim at the other. Dick put in his buck, the fur flew, the rabbits clawed at each other. He took the buck out and put it in next door. The same thing happened.

"How are you doing, Tim?"

"Well, master," said Tim, "they be clawing each other like wild cats."

"Perhaps it's love bites," said Dick.

"Not my idea of love bites, master." They stopped and took out the four mauled and exhausted bucks. The expert came down and, with a growing look of amazement on his face, turned the rabbits over one by one.

"You have 400 bucks here," he said. So that was the end of Dick's rabbit empire and the idea that I should join him in it.

We have been lucky to have the Dutton-Forshaws as neighbours. They moved in the year after me. The previous owner had grown thirty acres

They took out the four
mauled and exhausted bucks

of carrots, when carrots were unsaleable
and cabbages were sky high in price,
then thirty acres of cabbages when
cabbages were unsaleable and carrots
were sky high.

"He be a right flarsky (showy) farmer,"
said Alfred.

"Don't have anything to do with him
Master David", said Mrs. Mills.

Tim Meadows told of his end. A
creditor drove up to the front door,
and the owner ran out of the back,
jumped into his Land Rover and was
never seen again. The bank took over
everything.

Now I called on the middle aged
married couple who, I had been told,
had moved in. A pretty smiling girl

answered the door.

"Oh hello, can I see your father", I asked.

"You mean my husband", replied the girl trying to look grown up.

Over the years they have changed their bare "drainpipe house", sitting by itself in a field into a friendly country house surrounded by trees, daffodils and stables.

★ ★ ★

The weather to a farmer is not just important, it is the main concern of his life. Arthur Bryant writes that the reason England has started each war badly and ended triumphant is because, over three thousand years of changeable weather, the English farmer has gone out each day prepared to cope with the unexpected. The European farmer, on the other hand, has known what the weather is going to be like next day and has even been able to make a plan for some weeks ahead. Because of this Europeans probably do not have the inbred flexibility of mind of the Englishman.

★ ★ ★

When hail strikes a fruit farm it is devastating both for owner and man. In 1958 we had an excellent crop and had just started picking when, on the afternoon of September 5th, the black clouds piled high and the hail crashed down upon us. It was so heavy that instead of bouncing on the grass each hailstone buried itself in the ground. Along its hundred mile long and narrow path the hail killed cats, dented cars, crashed through greenhouses and even made holes in corrugated asbestos roofs.

we had just started picking when the hail crashed down on us

It was the worst hailstorm since 1840. The hailstones weighed out at five to the pound.

A week before the storm, a neighbour had been on television. He was a glasshouse grower and had remarked that unlike other farmers he was immune to weather changes. Perhaps the gods heard him; within a week he did not have a pane of glass left. All his crops, uninsured of course for hail, were ruined. It was a terrible blow.

Every apple on the farm was ruined. The hail sliced through them. It even damaged the bark of the trees, going right down to the wood underneath. When I met the staff next morning they could not look at me. They did not express any sympathy but they were all desperately upset.

We were in the middle of Worcester picking when the hail struck, and the pickers spent the next three weeks knocking off damaged apples with sticks. It was tempting to save the money but if left on the apples would have gone rotten and brought canker to every bough. I was lightly insured and

79

received £3,000. Still it helped.

Hail damage, however slight, is always worse than one at first hopes, while frost damage, quite devastating at first sight, in the end tends to be slightly better than feared.

This was our first brush with the weather. Next year we had a magnificent crop but it rained for the last time in May. It did not rain again until October except, thank heavens, for a thunderstorm early in August. We had been out playing tennis to the north when we saw the massive clouds gathering across the greensand ridge. As we raced home with our hearts in our mouths we realised that it had not been a hailstorm. There were no tattered leaves and small branches on the roads. When we got back we saw we had had two inches of rain in under half an hour. The trees had been desperate for water and this storm saved our crop. Earlier the trees had done what they could to save moisture; they had closed their stomata, curled in against the heat and shed surplus leaves. When the rain came they sucked it in. Within two hours you could see the change and as I stood in the middle of the orchard I could almost hear the water being pumped up and out to every part of the tree.

A Cox apple grows in diameter, if regularly supplied with food, water and warmth, at about half a millimetre a day. There are about a hundred and twenty days of growing between blossom and harvest. In severe drought the growth rate drops to about one millimetre a week but after this rain storm the apples put on about ten millimetres in seven days. They did not split because they were clean of scab and russett so the skins were flexible, We felt our troubles were over, but they were not. The drought came back and it didn't rain and it didn't rain and it didn't rain. We tried desperately to irrigate from our one tap, six trees a day was all it would do but it seemed something.

The drought continued and the trees shed a second lot of leaves; they had already shed one lot in July, and now they tried to make do with perhaps half their proper quota. Finally these leaves too gave up the struggle and by mid

September the trees were almost bare. They had done their best for us and we picked a fair crop of rather undersized apples.

Still day after day, the devastating heat continued. Apples were stacked everywhere. Along the drive up to the house boxes were placed six high and eight across; they curved like a small part of the great wall of China. We had no cold storage and our graders were only clearing three hundred boxes a day. The lightest girl helper spent each day walking along the top of the wall of boxes. She had to tread delicately where the corner posts of four boxes joined and gave a precarious foothold. She carried with her a hose, and hour after hour she watered the apples in order to stop evaporation. However much she watered, our apples were still losing weight and texture. Day by day the level in each box was visibly lower.

I remember the girl well. When she was leaving she said to me in hushed and wondering tones:

"I am going to INDIA." She made it

sound like the moon.

She was one of the first; it was before the days of the hippie run. She was startled to hear I knew India well and spoke Urdu.

We sold our apples in the end but I had learned two bitter lessons — a cold store and irrigation were essential. That drought was our second clash with the weather. It was the driest summer since 1745 — that is long before the French Revolution.

A. P. Herbert wrote

"The farmer is a peculiar man
He keeps his heart in his boots
For either the rain is destroying his
grain
Or the drought is destroying his roots."

It is quite true; the weather is wrong for us about three quarters of the time.

Not only had that drought and heat hurt our farm, but I had borrowed money to back a play called 'Caught Napping'. It had been written by Geoffrey Lumsden with whom I had been at Repton. It was the funniest play I have ever seen and I owned a tranche of 5%. It had been put on by Peter Bridge who lived locally. Few people go to the theatre when the evening temperature is over 80°F. The actors, the management and the author played fair by the 'angels' and all took a cut in pay but the play was slowly driven to the wall. It left me another £2,000 down the drain. How I hated that summer of heat and sun. That was the second year when it had needed all our strength to carry on —

"Does the road wind uphill all the
    way?
Yes to the very end.
Will the days journey take the whole
    long day?
From morn to night my friend."

Now in 1991 with two great frosts in
two years that road still winds uphill.

★ ★ ★

The first year that we had a big crop
I had not got together enough pickers.
It still nags me that I picked £15,000
worth of fruit and another £10,000 worth
fell on the ground. Money once lost
can never be recovered. To try and
save the crop, on Sundays I brought
in thirty schoolgirls from St. Michaels
School, near Petworth. They came in
chattering and laughing, We separated
them as far apart as we could, one from
the other. I and my foreman patrolled
ceaselessly. Gradually as the day wore
on the chattering died down and a new
attitude took its place. Those who were
good pickers began to enjoy the work

in the sun. I scattered praise and blame about. Alfred looked at each one and, if they were picking well, grunted. If they had only known a grunt was high praise indeed. If they were picking roughly he came and told me about it.

"That thar girl be rough as a gamoik", I never learned what a gamoik was.

As they quietened the mistress was delighted. We had the girls the next two weekends and the outing became popular. I was paying them the proper rate for the job and it must have seemed quite a lot. I blacklisted three or four girls who were not allowed to come again and that made the job more of a privilege.

With all these efforts however we were still picking on October 31st. The crop was a failure through lack of planning; good money lay bruised and rotting on the ground. The farm smelt of cider.

The next year I began to collect pickers six months in advance. I appointed an agent in the Storrington area who had worked for me during the year. Mrs. Diana Beaumont is now the Dame of Sark, or rather the wife of the Seigneur. She scoured the council estates and when

That thar girl be rough as a gamoik

picking was due we sent vans and cars in various directions. The whole success of a fruit farm depends on the pickers and if somebody works hard and earns a lot of money, good for them. One must not grudge it.

In the early days we paid on an hourly rate plus a bonus per box picked. This bonus needed a great deal of bookkeeping, but was very worthwhile and it showed up the lazy ones. An American girl, apparently eager and enthusiastic, bounded off to the place I had allocated her. At the end of the day the records showed that she had picked six boxes.

"Marilyn," I said, "our records must be wrong. They show you as having picked hardly any boxes. How many did you do?" "I think it was between twenty-six and thirty," she replied.

Looking through the records that evening I thought I would check up. Next day was warm and sunny and she was working at the far end of the farm. I walked quietly down and there she was stretched out in the sun, stripped to her bra and pants, sunbathing. She was off the farm within the hour. It was an accepted theory of fruit growing that if you put people on piece work they would rush the job and damage the apples. On time work they are paid from the moment they sign on to the moment they sign off. As I watched some of them trundling happily across the farm, pushing prams and chatting to their friends, all on my time, I decided to switch to piece work, We set a generous rate and once it was explained to them that, if they picked

She was off the farm within an hour

carefully, they could earn well over the
hourly rate, they scurried out of their cars.
The same mothers who had chatted and
trundled so slowly two days before were
shouting at their children.

"Hurry up, Sid. No, you can't go to
the toilet. I told you to do it before you
came."

Every new apple picker gets a brief talk
known by the staff as the Egg lecture,
It starts "Apples are more valuable than
eggs and are far more easily damaged."

To control pickers you need to
have energetic, amiable and intelligent
supervisors. Few supervisors are prepared
to be sufficiently strict with the bad
picker. That job comes back to the
boss. I am informed and I catch the
offender as he comes in next morning.

No you can't go to the toilet

Apples are more valuable than eggs and are far more easily damaged

"Your apples from yesterday show finger bruising. Please remember you must lift them gently, put them gently in the basket and release the skirt gently. If you bruise again you will have to go and we won't pay you for your day's picking."

I normally get a counter attack.

"Those apples can't have been mine, I've been ever so careful."

"I'm quite sure they are yours; we checked four boxes all with your numbers in, and they all show finger bruising and a few also show drop bruising,"

One can tell by the appearance of the

bruises how they are caused. The picking buckets, bags or aprons used now are much the same design as those used four hundred years ago, and shown in ancient illustrations. When the bag is full, the skirt, which is held up by a hook or string, is gently released and the apples flow out slowly from the bottom of the bag.

Some people, however well intentioned, cannot pick apples. Gypsies, who are quick workers, are either good or very bad. I was taking on two gypsies when another apple grower came to see me. He is a successful man tending to understatement. He watched me sign them in and hand them over to a supervisor.

"When I last saw that couple," he remarked, "he was running for his life towards me. His wife was after him with a 12-bore. She missed him with the first barrel."

"What happened then?" I asked.

"She dropped him at my feet with the second barrel. They seem to have made up the quarrel."

she dropped him at my
feet with the second barrel

They certainly worked well for me except for their habit of lighting fires on the orchard floor to cook their meals.

Piece work, while it brought with it a great improvement in speed and economy, led to unexpected side results, One woman would come in early before anyone else and, instead of staying in her own cant, would rush to pick all the easy apples in the neighbouring cants. Later she would deny having done so, Cant is Sussex dialect for a measurable job, e.g. a line of hoeing.

Another, who up to then had been a reliable picker, I found up a ladder throwing her apples down on to the grass. She then picked them up, all bruised, into the boxes. I was very angry indeed. She changed her ways and stayed with us for several years.

A well known grower asked me to take on his son as a trainee. His father had helped me a great deal so I accepted the boy and went to considerable trouble to find him lodgings with a pleasant family nearby.

I had not realised he was unbalanced. Each Saturday I gave him an hour's discussion on the farm's progress. I later found that he was repeating to the staff everything confidential I had told him. Then his landlady telephoned me. "John has asked for a reduction in rent. He says he will economise by not having baths".

"That's ridiculous. I'll speak to him."

"John," I said later that day, "you have asked Mrs. King for a reduction in rent. If you are going to stay there you must have a bath each day."

"You don't understand," he replied, "baths take the oil off your skin, they are bad for you as well as being expensive."

A few days later, during the coffee break, he threw a handbill (a small chopper) at one of my men. It missed the man but John had to go.

Three years later his father retired and sold up. On the day of the sale John hanged himself from an apple tree in the orchard; the poor father found him swinging there.

★ ★ ★

In the 1950s the only spray we had for codling moth was lead arsenate. We put this on twice a year, normally on about 15th June and then, for the second generation, three weeks later. It was a really dangerous spray to men and insects and we apple growers pressed the research stations to find something safer. The problem with spraying is to have something that kills the bug you are after but yet does not kill the other insects. Lead arsenate killed everything stone dead. As a result it was often followed by devastating attacks of red spider because, while it had killed the live spiders, it did not kill their eggs. These then hatched and there was nothing left alive to eat them. Friendly insects are the ladybird, the black kneed capsid, the lace wing and others.

The gradual 'greening' of apple growing began long, long before the general public ever thought of it. We used, four days after blossom fall, to put on twenty ounces per acre of a chemical to kill sawfly. This spray, however, also killed any bees which were unwise enough to visit the fruit trees after the blossom had gone. Bees can for a few days still get honey out of petalless blooms. We gradually reduced this down to ten ounces, then to five ounces, to two ounces and now it is very rarely used because of the danger to the bees and the beneficial insects.

There used to be an attitude of bravado among experienced fruit men. They considered wearing protective clothing and helmets as rather wimpish. Long before it was legally necessary we brought protective clothing into regular use. Certainly in thirty-five years of growing we have never had anyone, except possibly myself, even slightly affected by spray, I do not know of anyone in England who has over the last thirty-five years been incapacitated by fruit spraying. This is rather extraordinary when one thinks that early on we put on dangerous winter washes by hand lance. These, if they splashed onto the skin, turned it a dirty yellow.

Many years later, as soon as he came into the business, my son insisted that we cut our spray rates by two thirds and that we bought a cab tractor with a charcoal filter which purifies the air breathed by the driver. This has been a great pleasure for everyone. Men are able to spray all day without wearing oilskins and without getting dirty. The irritating thing is that by law one still has to wear oilskins for mixing up the spraying materials, even though we use only those of low toxicity.

As one walks through an orchard one is conscious day by day of the changes in the appearance of the leaves. Trees can look windblown — I don't believe they grow at all in a strong wind. The thirsty look is obvious because the leaves curl slightly in an effort to stop the evaporation of water. The slightest trace of powdery mildew can be seen by the faint silvering of the newest leaves. A shortage of nitrogen shows itself in a lack of dark green colour in the older leaves. Magnesium deficiency can be detected in leaf blotches and early leaf fall. A lack of lime shows up as manganese toxicity which causes the bark to be rough.

Some growers are very sensitive to the appearance of their trees. We had one who lived near us who had no sense of taste or smell: all his senses seemed to be in his eyes and his fingers. He was usually three or four days ahead of anyone else in knowing that the trees were off colour. He put so much intensity into his growing and nothing else that he sickened of it and suddenly upped sticks and went to Australia, where he now mows lawns for a living. He cropped his apples on branches growing between 35° and 55° to the flat. As a result he never had any small apples. It is a system which has never been properly researched.

Spraying has various objectives. The

simplest is spraying for insect damage. We have now been able to cut that down to one spray for both caterpillars and aphides and two sprays for codlin. In the old days aphides were very difficult to kill and one could only get them in the two days after they had hatched and before the bud opened. For caterpillars one sprays when the base leaves on the buds are the size of a finger nail. The second objective is to give nutrients to the leaves. For that purpose we spray three times a year with Epsom salts to give them magnesium and also frequently with small doses of urea for nitrogen, seaweed extract for trace elements and calcium which is badly needed by growing apples. Guano would be excellent but is not available.

The third objective is to stop scab and powdery mildew spreading. That is the difficult one and we spray three or four times early on to protect the emerging young leaves against the attack of fungus spores. If the spores fail to get an early foothold on the leaves one can stop spraying early. We would like to go organic, but I notice that apple trees in private gardens, while they get into balance with insects and rarely suffer from them are normally a mass of scab, mildew and canker. Organic apples at the moment are impossible to grow properly, but it may come. Organic vegetables, wheat and cattle are simple by comparison. My cousin down in Devonshire — Roger Cardain-Jones — has been growing like this for thirty years with great success.

There is usually little problem with insects in well managed corn, and in the right areas the problem of the fungus diseases of rinkasporium in wheat and eyespot in barley can be dealt with by companion planting. A dredge crop of oats and barley planted close together has few problems with fungus diseases. The Chinese have been using companion planting for thousands of years and there you will find rows of rhubarb, maize, potatoes etc all close together. It solves such problems as club root and indeed is not unlike the system used in well managed vegetable gardens. Compost seems to be the key to health and we remember that always on our farm and that is why we grow grass between the trees.

★ ★ ★

After the ferocious hail of 1958 and the terrible six month drought of 1959 we were stretched to the limit, but we had to have a cold store. We built this in 1960 and completed it on September 28th, but did not have time to get in the hard standing in front of the doors. That year it rained as it has never rained before or since and the tractors were only able to move by having wire cages attached to their wheels. These stick out three feet on either side and are far more efficient than chains. The tractors, throwing up waves, pulled the trailers like sledges through a two foot deep sea of mud. To get the fruit to the cold store we used a roller conveyor for the last thirty yards. My son Richard aged four stood for hours pushing the boxes along.

"Them there apple boxes be cledgy with mud," said my foreman, "I disremember it being so rainified since I be a nipper".

Alan, who had moved in during a rain

storm, coughed and smoked, coughed and smoked and looked smaller and more frail every day, but I realised that he was reducing all our burdens by inventing easier ways of moving the 150 tons we had to handle three times to get it into the cold store.

We sold the apples reasonably well and were about to put in irrigation the following spring when a frost took 75% of the crop in one night and we were forced to delay all capital expenditure.

Alan, proved to be rather an Eyore. When we had a fog in March he shook his head sadly.

"Fog in March, frost in May," he said and was proved right.

"Three years close together," he went on, "That's the run for frosty weather," but that saying was not fulfilled.

I don't disremember it being so rainified since I be a nipper

4

The Turn of the Tide

THE next year saw the turn of the tide for us. For seven years we had been struggling all the way, never without some unpaid bills and never without the pressure of something expensive and urgent to be done on the farm.

It is hard, now that better times have gone again, to remember what it feels like to have a really profitable crop. The year of 1962 was such a one. We had, with Alan's help, got our grading together. The picking went well and all the time we were harvesting, fifteen people in the grading shed were churning out over a thousand boxes a day. I took over from Alan in the evening and the campers worked till 10.00 at night and all day on Sunday. Three helpful friends of ours came in on rota to supervise. The lorries and the vans were moving out day by day to markets all over England.

The cheques began to come in; when Paula went down to our local bank the cashiers rushed to be first to serve her. The bank Manager came out and spoke to her.

"Is this all from apples?" he asked.

On one day she paid in over £17,000 from six different wholesalers.

I rang my main bank manager at Horsham about some problem.

"Before we talk, Mr. Atkins," he said, "I would like to tell you that your account is the most exciting one I have ever seen in all my life as a bank manager. Hardly any movement for six months and then suddenly money pouring in and out every week in thousands."

That month we paid off every bill and in a rash moment gave every member of staff a bonus of three months extra pay, which we repeated at Christmas.

At the end of the crop we had a visit from Robert Carrier. The apple industry had given him his first opening and employed him at about £4,000 per year to act as our public relations man. His success was due to having articles

103

of all dimensions ready at any time for any paper to print. An editor only had to telephone him and say "I have a space 8 inches by 12 inches, have you anything to fill it?" and he'd be round in a taxi with the copy within half an hour. From that start he discovered French colour photography of food and then he was away and flying high.

I saw quite a lot of him and invited him down to our house to speak to other apple growers. The timetable was tight and I met him at the station and brought him back to Tullens where we opened a tin of corned beef and fed him on that and a baked potato. He seemed to enjoy it.

Another visitor was the Editor of Vogue who, watching my pickers climb and bend asked.

"Do you have to pay them?"

"Of course".

"If I run an article 'Pick apples and slim, What the well dressed woman wears for apple picking', you could charge them £10 a day each," I never tried it.

★ ★ ★

We built Thorn cottage in 1960. It was entirely in Fittleworth stone and we had a good builder and a poor architect. The Sussex habit of tilehanging the first floor has one great disadvantage, one cannot grow plants up the house, they tear off the tiles.

This cottage was on the edge of Thorn common and reached by the old droving road which used to run from Pulborough market across the Arun to Wisborough Green. I learnt while building it that farm staff really prefer concrete type bungalows to houses.

When later we bought a second farm and planned to build two cottages we were looking for a new architect. I watched a lovely new house going up in West Chiltington and stopped and asked the name of the architect. He turned out to be a little round Jew, still in his thirties, who talked very fast.

"What a site, What a truly memorable site. The sweep of land, the distant Downs, what a site, what a house I will build you."

"Steady on," I said, "I only want a pair of cottages".

"A pair of cottages, but this site is fit for a noble house."

"The cottages should be built in an L shape. Three bedrooms and three small downstairs rooms each, bathroom upstairs, cloakroom downstairs."

"Very poky, no flow, no imagination."

"Please listen, I want it designed so the six bedrooms can turn into five, one staircase can come out and the six downstairs rooms can turn into four, with a big hall. All doors and floors to be good." I must have felt rich at the time.

"Now that is vision, that is imagination, that gives a challenge, that means" — he gestured widely.

He designed a stunning house in warm brick and with hand made tiles. We put it out to tender. Our local builder, Mr. Blake, amiable and renowned for the cheapness and sloppiness of his work, was easily the lowest. The architect and I discussed it.

"He cuts all corners, his concrete is largely sand, and his timber is unseasoned," I said. "If we accept, write and say we will insist on his keeping to the exact specification."

Keeping to the exact specification is a thing which even good local builders rarely do. They seem to go only on the plans and are hurt when specifications are mentioned. Mr. Blake came up to see me and waved the letter in my face.

"Keep to the specification," he said "I always keep to the specification. You know my work well."

I did indeed, the concrete yard that

he had installed had been put in by two cowboy builders and as it had no expansion joints had cracked badly. It still annoys me.

"I should warn you, Mr. Blake, that the architect will insist that everything is up to standard".

"Of course, of course, my work is well known around here." The digging of the foundations started. I went up to see it and was fingering with interest some pieces of old Roman tiles thrown up by the diggers when my next door neighbour, an elderly spinster and local JP, came out to see me.

"David," she said, "I have just been caught by Jeffery" (another neighbour) "poaching a pheasant on his land. Can I say I shot it on your land and was picking up a wounded bird?"

"But," I said, "You've no permission to shoot on my land."

"I know that, but I have been shooting your pheasants for years. I knew you wouldn't mind."

"But," I protested.

"But," she said, "I cannot as a JP be prosecuted for poaching. Surely you see that?" I weakly agreed.

The foundations of the cottage began to take shape. The architect went off with a sample of wet concrete. It was below standard.

Mr. Blake began to look thoughtful. He sent away one team of bricklayers and brought in a better one. The tiles arrived. The architect rejected them. The house continued to grow, but now the warm coloured brick was laid neat and clean and straight.

I'd paid two cheques when the row broke. I arrived at the site. Stout good natured Mr. Blake was almost in tears.

"But the wood, all that good wood will be spoilt," he cried.

The architect, all five foot two inches of him on his high heels, was waving the specification sheet and jumping up and down, "I told you, I told you," he said, "I told you the nails must be as specified. They must go in one millimetre below the surface."

"Why, why, what difference does it make?" wailed Mr. Blake.

"Your ordinary nails will not permit a sanding machine to clean the bedroom

I cannot as a JP be prosecuted for poaching. Surely you see that?

floors. All the floors must come out."

"My profit, what about my profit? What about my business? You will ruin me." He appealed to me. I referred him back to the architect.

Next day there was a pile of shattered wood outside the house and from inside came the squeak of nails being wrenched out from the beams to which they were attached. It was agonizing to hear. The splintered and nail marked wood was useless for anything.

The two cottages were finally built for £10,447. After twelve years I was forced to sell the farm and the new farmer used the architect's conversion to make one lovely house.

★ ★ ★

Our own house is long and low and lies within a stone wall which surrounds the garden. It looks bigger than it is. There are three houses of the same design in the area, Hardham Priory was built over 700 years ago; every room faces south with all the corridors to the north. This was copied in Coombelands Manor, built about 1750, on a smaller scale and then there is Tullens Toat which is the same design but again down in scale.

After our architect's success with Stile Place Farm we asked him to throw out a large bay window in our long narrow drawing room.

"It'll be a lovely room, a lovely room, but I must have a free hand, a free hand to choose my own builder. I am not going to have Mr. Blake." I doubted if Mr. Blake would ever come near him again. We gave him a free hand and three elderly craftsmen turned up. This was going to be their last job before retirement.

They would give no estimate.

"We won't be druv," said the eldest, "but we surely won't fornicate".

"Fornicate," I said in astonishment. They were all approaching seventy.

Three elderly craftsmen turned up

"Fornicate," cut in the architect, "in Sussex means to waste time".

"Oh really," I replied, thinking that that's why some jobs were so slow in Sussex. They were out fornicating.

The stone mason curved and shaped the stone, the carpenter put in a lovely long curving bench seat and the decorator put on the rich paper in the drawing room so carefully that it has now lasted twenty years, and as far as I'm concerned, looks to last another twenty.

Certain purchases in life always give one pleasure, and certain purchases with which you're stuck always give one pain. I never go into the farmyard without seeing the cracked concrete and I never walk round the front of our house without seeing the beautifully shaped stone of the bay window.

★ ★ ★

I had not yet realised that unused land is valuable for all wildlife and indeed I was still at the stage when I thought all the farm must be used productively and no part of the asset must be wasted. I had taken over about twenty-five acres of woodland and also, as Lord of the Manor, eight acres of Thorn Common which was thick with thorn trees under old oaks.

The seven acres of the oak wood which had been used by Canadian troops had been spoiled by them. When a tree grows it encapsulates anything like a nail which in the end becomes invisible. The metal lurks there, however, and when the oak is finally felled to be cut into planks, the great saws turning at high speed can be badly damaged by even one nail. On advice from the Forestry Department I cut half the wood at a time and found a contractor who would use the oak as fencing posts. As the oak is split with wedges this does not entail the use of a saw. Only some oaks are suitable for splitting.

I was eager to get on with replanting the cleared area and I chose, on the advice of the Forestry Department, spruce. Norway spruce is the Christmas tree and I planted it at the ridiculously close spacing of six foot by three. I had not realised what a terrible rod I was making for my back.

The trees were so close that no cutting machine could possibly get down between them. The land had to be hand cleaned with swap hooks.

To begin with we all went down in the heat of the afternoon and, bent double and stripped to the waist, with flies and horseflies all around us, we trimmed away the weeds from those horrid little trees. On the first day after four hours I knew that it was too much for us to do more than three hours at a time, and only then in the cool of the morning. It was a terrible job and for that reason I had to turn up myself on every occasion, If I did not, the work dropped considerably in speed. I only did one row to Alfred's two but I certainly learned how to sharpen a swap hook and use a hooky stick.

In those days I had a tendency, brought from the business world, to make advance budgets. This is useless because nothing goes to plan in farming. Nevertheless, having planted some thirty thousand trees, I quickly converted them in my mind to Christmas trees at a shilling a foot. I was as ignorant on this as on everything else. I had no idea that the

Christmas tree trade was then in the hands of villains.

If the trees grow well you can sell the largest of them the second year. But there was the problem of marketing. By now I knew the London markets well and I easily found wholesalers prepared to accept the trees. We dug them up, tied them into bundles often, piled them onto a lorry and sent them off. The driver was used to taking my apples and, because he had developed good connections with the porters, was usually unloaded quickly.

When however, he went up with a load of Christmas trees, lorries jammed themselves in front of him, opening the way for other lorries with Christmas trees to go ahead. The first day he did not get unloaded at all but came back with all the trees. By then we had dug a second load so we sent them both off to another market, where more or less the same thing happened. This time he did at least get unloaded, but the return we got was pitiful. Trees for which the public were paying the then quite respectable price of three to five shillings each, were sold by us for fourpence to sixpence, from which we had to deduct the commission and the market charges. We were being manoeuvred out of the market.

The following year I decided to sell direct and I advertised in the local paper. Several people rang me up and I interviewed a number of them. We walked through the Christmas trees and discussed grades, sizes and prices. Three people quoted. All of them put in firm prices and I accepted the highest for delivery on December 15th. On that day we had the trees waiting but no buyer turned up. I rang up the second man.

"Of course, Guv," he said, "I'd be pleased to take them."

He couldn't come that day; he would come in two days' time. I agreed the time and the price over the telephone with him and we again laid the trees out ready for collection. No lorry turned up, so when evening came I rang the third man.

"It's a pleasure, Guv," he said, "I would be prepared to help you out. Price is down the drain though."

By now it was December 20th. He was due to arrive at two o'clock in the afternoon but I got a telephone call in

the morning saying that he would come next day.

"I'll help you out Squire, but it's hard to give 'em away this year, but I'll tell you what I'll do to be fair. I'll give you half."

I had no alternative but to accept his offer. He turned up, then he said that the price had dropped further. He knocked off another ten per cent.

"Load them up, Guv," he said, "and I'll give you cash as soon as they are on." By this time I had the measure of my man, even if it was too late.

"I'll load them," I said, "when you have paid me."

He gave me cash, but the final result was that I got about twenty per cent of the original price. I had to accept, after Christmas a tree has no value. I am sure that the three people who quoted for the trees all knew each other, and that when the lorry was out of sight they met somewhere and divided the trees between them. It was a bitter lesson. The Christmas tree market in those days was rotten through and through, This was unlike the fruit market which was honest, surprisingly honest.

Those two disastrous years of trying to market Christmas trees had broken my will. I would allow the others to grow on to be proper trees. Out of every thousand trees we had originally planted we had dug up five hundred in the first year and another two hundred and fifty in the second, but we still had to continue to weed the rest. It took us another three years of hand work before they were well above the weed level and we could let them begin to look after themselves. Next the silver birch, which is very quick growing, became the problem, and every three years they and the old chestnut coppice had to be cut down. This continued until the spruce reached about ten feet. We got one commercial thinning from them at fifteen feet and then they were away, growing fast and looking splendid.

They had reached some thirty feet high when, in October 1987, came the hurricane. In one hour they were all scattered in a tangle. They didn't fall in rows. They broke or fell one across the other like spillikins; you could not walk through the wood. It was a terrible sight and, because so many other plantations had gone down on the same night, the timber was unsaleable. I took some bad advice from one of the merchants, who said they were no use at all and I set fire to the lot. The needles of the fir trees burned, and so did the small branches, but the main trunks didn't. They were, however, blackened and ruined for the paper market which emerged about two years later. Finally I had to get in a contractor to pile them all into vast bonfires.

This situation, which in my case was only a few acres, was repeated all across the south of England. The countryside will not recover from the 1987 hurricane for at least a hundred years.

I have now started again with oak and ash. Perhaps these trees have a greater chance because there has been a striking development in forestry. Before, to protect the tree from rabbits, one had to put rabbit wire all round the plantation, but now one can put a tube round each tree. The cost in 1989 of planting each tree with the tube and stake was about one pound, of which the tree itself represented some 15p. They are not merely fully protected from rabbits but, to some extent, from deer. Deer have an irritating habit of eating the tops out of both forest and fruit trees. If only they would eat the branches I wouldn't grudge it to them, but they go for the growing point, which at a certain time in the tree's life is at the level of their heads. The tree is then completely ruined.

After the 1987 hurricane there were two summers of extreme drought, I planted in the winter of 1989 in time for the drought of 1990, I am not sure how many of the trees have lived, but I think probably about seventy per cent have come through, We planted at twelve foot square and can get a tractor with a masher through between the trees. This will stop the onset both of weeds and the ubiquitous silver birch.

The oak and the ash are natural trees and are a good habitat for all the insects, animals and birds. A tree that is extensively planted and is not friendly to England is the horse chestnut. Unfortunately, to replace my dead elms, I planted an avenue of these trees before I realised that they were foreigners.

When we came to Tullens, apart from the avenue, we had seven or eight large elms behind the house. These sheltered us from the north winds, and were a pleasure and a protection. We watched with horror when in the seventies the elm tree beetle rampaged through them. All the elms in the county were killed. It changed the whole face of the countryside. Has the disease died out now? We have a few new young elms which have come again and have not yet been killed but what happened to the beetles? Did they die in their millions as their food supply ran out? England was lucky they were unable to change over to oak or ash. Normally insects can alter their eating habits.

From the hurricane of 1987 we learned that the oak is not as strong a tree as we thought. Its branches were frequently twisted and broken off. The sturdy oak of England, which would stand against any blast, was a delusion.

★ ★ ★

We had still not put in irrigation and after the terrible drought of 1959 we knew we had to have it. Fortunately I had a pump on the river and this had a three quarter inch pipe leading up to the main farm a mile away. This pipe used to be the main supply to the farms it crossed and it was their legal responsibility to maintain it and the pump, both of which were now unserviceable. In exchange for relieving them of this responsibility they gave me a right to put a four inch pipe across the land, and a new electric pump on the river. The river floods regularly so the pump had to be located at the maximum height of its pulling power. This has been a great disadvantage. Once the water is up to the pump it can easily be pushed up the next hundred feet to a small reservoir which we made in the bluebell dell in Lions Copse.

At vast cost we ordered the pipes in aluminium, When they were due to arrive I expected several lorry loads of them. Aluminium is very light and it all turned up on one six ton lorry and was easily unloaded by hand. It didn't seem worth the money.

The aluminium pipes were in thirty feet lengths and as they kept on breaking apart at the joints we had to patrol the long line. When a break was found one switched off the pump, put the pipes together again and then switched on the pump, It sounds easy but might involve walking or running half a mile or more. It needed a pair of walkie talkie telephones which at that time were not available.

Meanwhile to get across the road we had to get permission to build two scaffold towers which carried the line higher than the highest possible lorry, The following year we were able to put the pipes underground across the fields and the road and right up to the reservoir, From there we can, with a large diesel, pump water to anywhere on the farm, The diesel is not as good as an electric pump, but there is no electric line near.

The electric pump on the river has been there ever since. Watching it work it still amazes me that 250 gallons a minute is passing through it, hour after hour, almost soundlessly, We filled the reservoir with tench and two sorts of carp which were supplied free by the River Board. The carp have grown to about two feet in length, and many have been caught and returned. The reservoir is also home to moorhens. These attractive birds, so like the coot except for the colour of their beaks, are death to ducks. If a duck hatches out its eggs nearby the moorhen will, in order to protect its pond, sneak up behind the line of ducklings and drown them one by one. The parent ducks do not appear to notice.

★ ★ ★

One of the nicest workers I ever had was Bill Young. One sees so much of the staff on a farm that those to whom it is always a pleasure to talk are esteemed and cherished. Bill was cheerful and obliging. He scurried round his tractor like a terrier, always eager to be away.

"Lovely day sir, no time to waste sir, must be off, sir."

"That there Bill," said Alfred, watching him, "will one day run hisself over with the tractor he be driving. He be in two places at same time."

Basil Furneaux had spoken of the three types of tractor driver.

"The first puts in diesel and is off. He never checks anything. The second checks everything, always finds something wrong and spends an hour or more putting it right. By the time he starts the weather has changed and it's too late. The unusual man gets away at once when it's urgent. He checks his tractor thoroughly only when there is ample time. Treasure him."

★ ★ ★

In 1971, in the National Apple Register, 6000 varieties were recorded, these were known by over 16,000 local names, Now the National fruit collection at Brogdale has 3551 of these in its collection, few of which are worth growing except for genetic material, and under one thousand are in use.

When I had been apple growing for about five years I felt I should bring in some of the old varieties. I consulted Basil Furneaux and on his advice planted Orleans Rienette, Tydemans Late Orange, Heugans Golden Rienette and Blenheim Orange. They were all a commercial disaster, The Tydemans Late Orange has a beautiful flavour but the apple is too small to sell well; the

Blenheim Orange doesn't crop for ten years and both Rienettes fall off just before they are ready to pick. Over nearly forty years of fruit growing I have watched apple after apple come and go. Others I have planted have been Fortune, a good flavoured apple which falls off too early; Scarlet Pimpernel which becomes smothered in mildew and George Cave which cracks on the tree. This last is the earliest apple we have ever sold commercially and, for some four days, but only for four days, has a lovely flavour. Pick it and it looks perfect, but as the box is lifted on to the trailer there will be a 'crack' and another apple has split.

The Egremont Russet lasted longer with us but it is on the tree one day and on the ground the next. It was a dreadful thing in the evening to walk through an orchard of George Cave and hear them split or five weeks later into an orchard of Egremont Russet and hear them fall plop, plop on the ground. Egremont Russet is also very likely to suffer from enlarged lenticels which look like blackheads on a pimply boy. To cure this you need

The Egremont Russet is likely to suffer from enlarged lenticels

to spray again and again with calcium nitrate — not calcium chloride which scorches their leaves.

Fruit growers are frequently criticised for not growing the old varieties. There is only one reason why we do not do so: the public won't pay enough for them. They may perhaps buy a few pounds of an old variety, but in a shop full of ten varieties of apples the purchases will be approximately in the proportion of fourteen Cox's to four Bramleys to two of the other varieties.

Recently I was at Lord Selborne's show of a hundred and twenty old varieties. I had myself grown many of those which were most presentable and which had a good flavour, but the others are well lost except perhaps for breeding. There was an elongated apple called Sheep's Nose which had no attraction and there were Costards and many ribbed apples, ugly and unattractive. The Lord Lambourne apple was there; it has a lovely flavour but its harvest time comes in the middle of the Cox season and we have to pick the tree four times to get the colour. One day an apple may have a mauve tinge and is unsaleable, two days later the mauve has turned to scarlet and that apple is ready for picking, while other apples deep in the centre of the tree are still tinged with mauve.

At one time I started The Apple Shop in Knightsbridge. There I stocked never less than ten varieties, but it was not commercially successful and I had to give up. It was finally killed by the Post Office. I had orders for four thousand Christmas boxes and sent them off, but many of the apples arrived bruised in the postal rush and I had to give refunds, I am sure that the postal staff threw the parcels from pile to pile.

From the grower's viewpoint Cox, apart from its excellent flavour, has the great advantage that it does not fall off before it is due to be picked. What we need is a Cox that crops as heavily as a Golden Delicious or a James Grieve, both of which we use as pollinators.

Most apple trees have to be pollinated by another tree. A few trees, such as Bramley, are sexually impotent and in such an orchard, the pollinator itself has to be pollinated by a third tree.

One Worcester to eight Cox used to be the standard plant, but sometimes Worcester is a day or two late in which case the early Cox bloom may, even on a warm day, go unpollinated. To stop this we grafted a branch of James Grieve, a Casanova of an apple, onto each fifth tree. Nowadays we never plant less than two pollinators at a ratio of one to six.

The use of rootstocks to control the growth of trees goes back into prehistory. In the Middle Ages Paradise stocks were in use to keep trees small and through the next four hundred years many rootstocks were interchanged across Europe. In the early 1900's East Malling Research Station collected and classified 71 types in common use and from these in 1917 published their findings. In order of strength the best stocks were classified as MI, MII and MIX, the last being a small tree with roots as brittle as carrots which has to be staked all its life.

In the sixties more rootstocks were released and we all planted MM104 (A great failure), MM106, M26 and M27, the last two of which are related to MIX.

Shortly afterwards scientists found how to clear the viruses out of both rootstocks and trees and now there is a bank of mother trees from which all nursery trees take their original buds. A few nurseries have not played fair and I recently bought some Lord Lambourne trees which had the rubbery wood virus. With this virus each branch bends to the ground and the trees have to be burnt.

The effect of all the research has mostly been useful but we have more or less lost M2, which was a marvellous rootstock, and MIX, cleared of its inbuilt virus restrictions, is now growing too big.

All over the world apple growers owe a debt to East Malling, which largely founded by English growers, gave away their information free. Unfortunately this has helped our competitors to flood our market.

In 1983 we planted eight acres of three row beds which two years later won the prize for the outstanding young orchard in England. We were advised to pollinate the field, one in nine, with Golden Delicious. This variety never having done it before went biennial, that is it flowered every second year, In desperation we interplanted a variety of cheap trees as extra pollinators, but for three years we had to cut blossoms from other orchards and hang them, in 3000 milk bottles, on every third tree. The advisor advises but the grower has to cope with the result. We still employ this advisor, who was responsible for converting most growers from planting single rows into planting three rows together. This gives more trees to the acre and less land is used as alleyways.

For real pollination drama the Avocado tree can not be beaten. At sunrise all the male flowers open on one variety, At midday they close and ten minutes later the female flowers on the same tree open. To get any fruit, trees have to be put next to another variety where the female flowers open in the morning and the male in the afternoon. The main varieties sold are Fuerte and Haas; these are sexually compatible as their flowers open at opposite times. The Haas is the roundish avocado with a rough skin and with not so good a flavour as the smoother Fuerte.

A heart warming sound in the orchard on a windless, warm day is to hear the apples clicking. Stand still and listen. It comes from all around one — click, click — click, click. It is the noise of the growing apples changing their position so that they may have more space. The click is the quick movement of one apple across the skin of another.

A terrifying sound to hear is the frass (droppings) being evacuated by caterpillars as they munch away. I have only heard it once and that was not in my orchard. Anyone who hears it has failed disastrously in his growing.

5

Bees and Frost

IN 1962 when we first had caravanners we were innocents. In the Times and Telegraph, where I advertised for staff, I unwisely said we would pay the fare to the farm. As a result we were flooded with applications from Scotland. We booked them in from September 10th for a fortnight. When they arrived the crop was not quite ready, so we employed them in picking over the apples down to a diameter of $2\frac{1}{4}$ ins (60 mm). The campers worked hard and drank hard, but when they left most of the crop was still to be picked. We advertised again. We needed pickers quickly so we gave our telephone number. The calls came in thick and fast. The first man we had taken on rang back.

"May I bring my father?"

"Are you sure he's fit?"

"Oh, yes, never had a day's illness in

his life." The father arrived and had a mild heart attack on the second night. For two weeks our expensively hired caravan was taken up by the father with his son nursing him. We hadn't the heart to ask them to leave.

Our next applicant asked if she could bring her dog. She sounded so suitable we said yes. The dog turned out to be a fourteen year old labrador, deaf and with a hearing aid. He lay in the caravan making appalling smells. The other three occupants complained bitterly, but instead of sacking the woman we were stupid enough to hire another caravan.

That year we took the campers in on a Saturday. The idea was to get them settled in on the Sunday. In later years we learned to take them in on Sunday evenings.

A deaf camper now arrived. He too had a hearing aid and oddly enough it was the same make as the dog's. With time to spare he enquired whether Sir Donald Blank lived nearby.

"I know a girl who works there as an au pair", he said.

I pointed him over the hill and in the afternoon, he walked across to

Sir Donald's house. Sir Donald was accustomed to drink at luncheon. The conversation went something like this.

"Can I see Mary?"

"Mary, Mary who?" asked Sir Donald.

The picker's hearing aid went on the blink and started to whistle.

"The girl who works here," he shouted.

"Girl, you want a girl. What do you think this is — a brothel?" I was telephoned by a cross Sir Donald.

"David, one of your staff is outside my door demanding women. He must be drunk. He can't hear a word I say and he's making an extraordinary whistling noise. Please come and take him away at once."

I went round and fetched the man, who then asked to borrow my car to go and buy some food. Foolishly I lent it to him and we learned later that he went off to Winchester, fifty miles away. We never lent cars again.

Among the others we had four Irish students. Dublin University was starting late that year and this group was charming. We were surprised after a week to be invited down there to dinner; we took down with us a couple of bottles of wine and had an excellent meal cooked by Siobhan, a pretty girl who always wore riding boots which she had bought at the local jumble sale.

When picking was over we were still grading and also needed men on the twenty acres of apples we were planting at our new farm, Stile Place. Three thousand chestnut stakes of $2\frac{1}{2}$ to 3 inches in diameter had to be hammered in, The men worked in pairs, swinging the heavy iron mallets alternately. In those days I could swing a mallet high over my head and hit a stake hard and true, but few of them could do so. They tapped away laboriously.

"It is too awful, sahib!" said a young Indian, "In all my deepest nightmare sleepings I never thought to do such horrid work, only fit for lowest coolie." He kept going, tapping away weakly with his mallet. Fortunately we did have two men who could swing a mallet hard and

hit a stake fair and square. They were invaluable.

At last the stakes were all in place and the camp paid off. The trees had not arrived. These cannot be lifted from the nursery beds until the leaves have released all their goodness back to the roots and fallen off. Lift them too early and the trees die easily.

In early December some members of the camp came back to plant. Through my ignorance we all made heavy weather of it and we did not finish until December 20th, when, with relief, I again paid them all off, Siobhan, the pretty little fair haired girl from Dublin, still wearing her riding boots, asked if she could stay on.

"No," I said, "you really should go back to your parents, You are away at University half the year and they will want to see you over Christmas."

"I can't go to my father's. I hate him, I can't bear him kissing me," she shuddered. "And I can't go to my mother's because if my father learns of it, and he will, he will cut off my allowance. If he does that I'll have to leave University."

She was a sweet girl, Siobhan, but I hardened my heart.

"We are certainly not having you living all by yourself in a caravan over Christmas. Our house is full, You must find somewhere you can go."

I took her down to the station, watched her buy a ticket, carried her bag under the tunnel across to the London platform, kissed her goodbye and watched her go.

It was a cold Christmas. The snow fell and the wind howled. In spite of our great log fires we had the massive central heating on. With twenty two ancient radiators the house creaked and groaned. To get to the shops we had to take a tractor across the unbroken snow sparkling in the sun and under the heavy laden trees.

As the snow rose the rabbits came in over the wire and attacked our newly planted trees. We cut off branches on the Home Farm and took them across by tractor and trailer to Stile Place, which was five miles off down a narrow lane. We laid the branches between the trees and the wood so the rabbits came to the

The snow rose high

branches first. They stripped off and ate the bark from the cut branches and for a few days left the trees alone. This gave us a respite to put anti-rabbit protective paint on the stems of the trees.

Then the snow rose higher and the rabbits, who had now eaten all the bark off the cut branches, were able to strip the main branches above the protective paint, and so we had to paint higher.

I have grown over the years to hate rabbits. There is no way to defeat them. We have been unfortunate to farm in the two great explosions of rabbits. The late 1950's and now, are the two greatest peaks in rabbit population ever.

When rabbits were regarded as a valuable source of food, they were farmed in warrens. It was the Normans who first built them brick burrows in which to shelter and from this, with the versatility of all survivors, they learned to make their own warrens.

It was during this fortnight that another local fruit farm was virtually wiped out by rabbits. When the London owner saw the murdered trees he sacked the manager on the spot. He was right to do so for during that cold spell the manager had stayed in his warm office bewailing the problem and doing nothing to save the trees.

One morning, after a fresh fall of snow, I was getting out the tractor when I noticed a small wisp of smoke coming from one of the caravans. I stumped across through the snow and inside found Siobhan, wrapped up in all the clothes she had, a blanket over her shoulders, holding her hands out to a tiny fire. She burst into tears when she saw me. After I had said goodbye, she had got off at the next station, bought herself as much tinned food as she could carry and had crept back to the caravan. For over a week of that bitter winter she had been living there without any light or heat. The day I found her she had been so cold she had lit a small fire to cook herself some soup.

"Please, please, can I stay," she said. "There are only four more days of the holiday and then I can go back to Dublin".

Paula had her into the house, fed her up, and off she went, as plump and pretty as ever. I told this story out at dinner one night to Nicky Byam Shaw who is now the Chairman of Macmillans. A few years later when he was taking on staff he realised that the fair Irish girl he was interviewing might be my Siobhan. On her CV was four months' work on an apple farm. "Did you ever work at Tullens Toat?" he asked.

"Yes," she replied and then went silent for a moment. Under his encouragement she went on:

"That Christmas was weird. I was so hungry and so cold and I could not go out of the caravan because of the footprints."

He gave her a job. Fair Siobhan, you are one of the few of five hundred campers whose face, tear wet and sweet, is still vivid to me.

* ★ ★

The new farm we had just planted was on the greensand ridge. It looked south across the flood plain to the South Downs and it was flat and yet high enough to be out of the frost. The ridge runs right across West Sussex and the easily worked soil has probably been in cultivation for over four thousand years. The Normans took over the big estates on it from the great Saxon lords. The Saxons were driven out to farm on the heavy clay of the Weald. The great estates still hold most of the ridge — Cowdray at Midhurst, Leconfield at Petworth, Barttelot at Stopham, then on to Parham and Wiston. Because of the heavy clay of the Weald there is not a great house north of the ridge until you come near Guildford. I had been lucky to get over twenty acres of this precious soil, and that for only £3,000. It had been badly farmed and was full of couch or quitch grass. If you break this up with cultivations, every separate bit of grass grows. The only way to clear the field is to drag out and burn such grass as you can and then cultivate three or four times at a weeks interval. The remaining couch tries to grow, gets disturbed, tries again, gets disturbed and with luck exhausts itself and dies. This we did with some success.

★ ★ ★

Apples are graded into first, second and damaged. It is illegal to sell the damaged on the wholesale market. In my early days I found a retailer in Worthing, Reginald Spells. He took all my damaged apples for 3d a pound, which would now be about one pence. He sold them at 4d a pound. There was always a queue for the damaged apples and as fast as they could two girls put them into paper bags. He was by far the best fruit retailer I have ever seen; he piled high and sold cheap. As the stocks ran out at the front counter more stocks were pushed through from hatches at the back.

There was always a queue for the damaged apples

Fruit and vegetables are so bulky that whether you are dealing with them in a packhouse or in a retail shop there must be a one way flow. Apples go in at one end of a packhouse and out at the far end, never crossing the line of the flow. If they do there may be confusion. Few retail shops have grasped this principle and one sees people carrying replacements through the selling area. Reginald Spells had solved this problem. He or one of his sons stood hour after hour watching from the supply area through the hatches as the vegetables and fruit flowed outwards from bulk store to counter and into the shopping bags, The tills were so placed that he could see them all and, as the staff had their backs to him, he could check whether anyone was fiddling. His shop must have had the highest turnover per square foot of counter of any in England.

When he was buying better quality apples from me he had an interesting technique. We would stand in the despatch area with hundreds of apple boxes of various grades around us. At random and with my permission he would tear off several paper covers.

"I think I can help you, Mr, Atkins, to clear some of these."

"Don't bother, the markets are clamouring for them."

It is always easy to sell first quality apples of $2\frac{1}{2}$ ins diameter, four to the pound, or of $2\frac{3}{4}$ ins diameter, but it is more difficult to sell those of over 3 ins diameter which weigh two to the pound, or to sell the ones of $2\frac{1}{4}$ ins diameter which weigh six to the pound. If a retailer knows four apples make a pound it is very quick to fill a bag. Spells used to home in on the less popular sizes and while we argued about the price he would pick up, apparently by chance, the two worst looking apples on the top of the box. He would not say anything, but would turn them over in his hand. Early on it would throw me.

"Perhaps those are a little below grade." I would say.

"There will be more of them further down in the box, we'd better knock a halfpenny off the price."

As we grew to know each other better, the transactions took place with little conversation except a certain amount of banter.

"You can't afford these," I would say, "They're too high a quality for your shop."

Forty years later his son still takes a very considerable quantity of apples off me. It took us fifteen years to reach Christian name terms and another ten before we ceased fixing prices. Nowadays he takes the apples and sends me a cheque, which is always fair.

These days over fifty per cent of all the apples in England are sold in supermarkets. Indeed thirty five per cent of supermarkets total gross profits come from the sales of fresh fruit and vegetables, although these account for only eighteen per cent of their total turnover.

★ ★ ★

Apple picking is rather like a campaign during a war, There is not enough time, communications fail, messages go astray, people are ill, tractors break down, wheels are punctured, lorries do not arrive and some vital item, such as a wheeljack, is mislaid. Throughout this shines, like the courage and dedication of one's soldiers, the cheerfulness and dedication of many of one's pickers. Stout Mrs. Dean, eighteen stone of sweating energy, determined to get the highest apple; sweet faced Mrs. Appleby, always smiling; Mrs. Chandler, day after day keeping the grading steady, the main staff working until dark to get the full boxes counted and collected and the pickers' places restocked with empty boxes for the next day. There are many pleasant memories. Mrs. Hamilton of Wisborough Green wrote to me when she returned to teaching:

"Thank you for the many fragrant and beautiful memories of sunshine, skins of rosy apples, mists and the perfumed air. It was a lovely experience — even the rain."

Running through it too are the ugly memories. The two yobs who beat a badger to death, skinned and ate it in their caravan. They were out of the camp as soon as I heard. The Irish nurse who, seeing I was under great strain, needled me with the intention of pushing me over the top. The trusted picker whose car boot we found loaded with stolen apples.

When we had three farms on the go at once there was no time to spare. We had only fifteen working days to pick those precious apples which were our livelihood.

As in wartime, sleep was very difficult and then, perhaps at two in the morning, the telephone by my bedside might go. A camper:

"I am stuck at Gatwick, could you please come and fetch me."

"Sleep the night there and come on in the morning."

"I haven't any money."

"Take a taxi and we'll pay at this end."

"There are no taxis."

"I'll send someone from the camp." So up I'd get to rouse someone from the camp.

When this happened I learnt to deduct the extra pay of the camper sent from that of the camper fetched home; this caused startled indignation, my purse was regarded as limitless.

But then again campers might go to considerable efforts to avoid bothering one. There was dear, pretty Michelle from South Africa (my wife loved her too) who, when she was quite ill, walked over a mile to a telephone to save disturbing us.

★ ★ ★

Bees are a lazy lot of lay-a-bouts. If the weather is cold they don't get up in the morning. When one has hired in forty hives at £10 each and placed them strategically throughout the orchards it is quite maddening to see that, by half

154

past ten on a cold morning, not one bee has emerged to work, The bumble bee with its furry coat is impervious to cold and gets out and about in all weathers. These brave insects nest in hedges; over the years I have become very fond of them and will always help them out from behind window panes and feed them honey if they are exhausted. They can now be bought, 30 bees to a hive, but they are expensive.

Another maddening habit of bees is that they tend to get hooked on one crop. Bluebells come out just before apple blossom and bees love them, as they do that yellow invader of the countryside, oilseed rape. Bees home in on rape, but from it they make poor honey with a bad flavour. This honey solidifies quickly in the hives and is difficult to harvest.

To stop the bees getting and staying on the wrong crop one can move them a minimum of five miles, as the crow flies, from their home base. If you then put them down in the middle of an orchard which is already flowering they may condescend to help with the apple blossom. If you put them there a day too early and before the apple blossom is producing nectar, they will be off to the nearest bluebell wood or rape field and return there each trip.

Even if they are put in the middle of an orchard with the blossom out and full of nectar they are quite capable of going for the dandelions in the grass. Dandelions lie so flat to the ground that they are very hard to cut with a mower, but as a routine one cuts the grass before the bees come in. When placing hives you put them facing into the sun and nowhere near another grower's orchard. You, not he, have paid for them and they are there to work for you. Hives are placed at night. It is a tricky job because, when moving them, their entrances have to be closed off with only enough grass to let in sufficient air for the bees to breathe but that grass must be in sufficiently firmly so that it doesn't fall out when the bee hives are bumping along on a trailer. Each hive has to be tied firmly with rope as otherwise the loose segments of which it is made may come apart. Fortunately bees cannot see in the dark and if a hive disintegrates one just has to switch off the lights and move away.

The spray we used to use for sawfly was death to bees and in those days it was vital to get all the hives out of the orchards before putting it on, Bees hate the smell of human sweat and anyone who doesn't bath properly is likely to be chased. One man was constantly being attacked but I never had the heart to tell him the reason, When a bee is attacking it has a higher pitched note to its flight. This is probably because it speeds up.

If attacked in daylight and there are trees nearby, run through them but never in a direct line. When one turns sharply the bee tends to fly straight on; it astonishes me that they can't turn corners easily. Bees tend to get bad-tempered if the hives are placed below electricity lines and also if the weather is cold in summer time. The days are few when the blossom is out, the nectar flows, the bees work and the grower can listen contentedly to the hum in the orchard as the apples are pollinated. Maddeningly I understand that bees in Australia work far harder, collecting honey by moonlight and producing four times the amount ours make.

I was lucky to have a Beemaster living near me. He was certainly a master of bees and was very fond of them. Mr. Wakeford — you must give countrymen their title — was a gentle giant of great charm. He lived at Wisborough Green in a wooden house which he had built himself. He told me he never slept more than one hour a night. He and I would go round together, I wearing mask and gloves and he wearing nothing on his hands and face. He would croon to them:

"Come on little fellows. Sorry I have to take your honey but I'll give you back some nice syrup."

Sometimes all the bees would line up along the edges of the supers (the tiers of honeycomb), all of them looking at us.

"They're just wondering whether to attack," he said, "I had better give them just a whiff of smoke."

With smoke from burning corrugated cardboard wafting across them they would turn down, back into the hive. We were never seriously attacked.

We were never attacked.

Honey is spun out of the supers by centrifugal force. First, however, the wax tops have to be sliced off all the cells, this is best done with a hot carving knife. The honey, thrown by the spinner out of the cells on to the spinner walls collects at the bottom and can then be run off into jars.

The bees, having had the fruits of their year's work stolen from them, will follow the trailer back and mark where it goes. House doors and windows must be well closed with no cracks for them to get through.

One evening after we had been spinning honey in the kitchen Paula and I went out. Ignorant as ever I opened a small window to let out the few bees which had crept in under the door. These bees raced home with the news.

"Come quick. We have found our stolen honey."

In the gloaming the bees came in their tens of thousands. They loaded up with honey from the supers standing there, and then, because it was now dark, could not find their way out. They were stranded.

When we got back home we heard the throbbing of a hundred thousand bees. After some thought we decided to risk it. I unlocked the door and with our coats over our heads we crept through the hall which was awash with bees. They hung in huge clusters on coats and on wellington boots, and were thick on the windows and the floor, As we opened the door into the main house bees poured after us, flying up the stairs and into the bedrooms. Our clothes were full of bees but none attacked.

I then took a tall standard lamp out of the front door onto the garden path, I switched it on and the bees streamed out of the wide open door onto the lamp. Their weight pulled it over and the bulb broke.

By now thoroughly frightened we crept up stairs and hid under the bedclothes. Bees flew around the bedroom all night. George, the Beemaster, was out at 6 o'clock in the morning. He looked in amazement at the scene and to our dismay drove back to get his camera. The bees were clustered, layers thick, on a window which faced the morning sun. This could not be opened; the bees were surging up the glass and as each layer reached the top, it fell back and started to climb again.

George was so busy admiring the scene and taking photographs that he was in no hurry to put us out of our misery. Eventually however he laid all the sticky hive components outside on the lawn and let the bees clean them up. He wore no protective clothing and had no objection to the 'little chaps' crawling all over him. By the end of the day most of our unwelcome guests had gone but we were still finding dead bees months later.

George later in his life was decorated by the Queen.

When looking after bees one must watch out that weeds and grass do not obstruct their flight path, that mouse guards are placed at the front of hives in winter, that unoccupied hives are protected from wax moth and that the entrances are too small for wasps to get in. Bees are not merely lazy but they are really very poor hands at looking after themselves.

In the summer empty decoy hives are put out. I am not good at taking swarms but on one occasion I was called round to a house locally. As I arrived the swarm, rather to my relief, took off. When I got home it had housed itself in one of my decoy hives.

We used to have the bees, clearly marked DANGER, near the strawberry fields. One day a boy of nine or ten wandered across, picked off the roof and started taking the hive to pieces. He was stung several hundred times. I ran up to the house and told Paula. While I telephoned our doctor, she rushed the boy round to the surgery. There seemed little chance of his living. One hour later, with the stings picked out of him, he was back on the strawberry field where his casual parents were still picking. He was one of those few people who have immunity to bee venom.

★ ★ ★

Frost during the spring is the great enemy of the fruit grower. When the bud scales begin to move the danger starts. The bud then puts out two tiny leaves which are known by the endearing name of 'early mouse ear'. At this stage damage can be done at between 7° and 5° of frost, which is 25° to 27°F. 'Mouse Ear' comes three days later followed by 'early green bud', 'green bud', 'early pink bud', 'pink bud' and finally 'full bloom'. At each stage the susceptibility of the bud to frost gets greater by half a degree Fahrenheit until at full bloom it can be killed by a four hour frost at 30°F. From then onwards the susceptibility of the apple decreases by approximately half a degree every three days. The period during which loss is likely to occur is from late March to the end of May. It is a long time to live on one's nerves.

Close friends of ours at Kirdford were made aware of this after a disastrous dinner party they gave for three apple growing couples one May.

When everyone had arrived and the red wine was open to breathe, two of the wives whispered that their husbands were on tranquillizers and were off drink. The third husband drank heavily and, fixing his host with a beady eye, talked only of frost.

The meal was disrupted when one of the growers went out on two occasions to consult a thermometer on the roof of his car. Each time he returned all conversation stopped while he gave his report.

In the middle of the pudding course he went out for the third time and returned to report a sharp drop in temperature. Two of the couples left at once, one to his smudge pots and the other to his frost sprinklers. Now no apple grower is ever invited to that hospitable house in May.

Dangerous frosts either occur on still

nights or with a slight northerly wind. Frost runs downhill and the difference in temperature between our house at 140 feet above sea level and the lowest field at 30 feet above sea level can be as much as 6°F. The flow of frost downhill is known as a katabatic wind. I have rather sticking out ears and on a still night I can feel this wind flowing past me at about half a mile an hour. As the frost moves downhill it flows not as freely as water but a good deal more freely than treacle. It cannot get through a rabbit fence but will go over it. It is important to give it a clear smooth path out of the vulnerable orchards down to the lowest fields which can never be planted with apples because of the frost risk. In early March we clear the frost gaps in the hedge close down to the ground and we cut the grass frequently. Even a tuft of grass or a small pile of prunings will throw an eddy of frost up into the trees.

There are three ways of protecting apples. The best is by spraying them with water throughout the frost. As the water on the trees turns to ice it will give out latent heat which will keep the

On a still night I can feel
this wind flowing past me

bud warm. This for the moment stops
the ice already formed from becoming
too cold but the supply of water must
be continuous. One needs a large pump
and water supply to keep the spray going
from about midnight until two hours
after sunrise. It is very difficult to protect
all the trees in a big orchard as one can
well use an inch of water per acre per
night. An inch to the acre is twenty-six
thousand gallons, and on fifty acres that
comes to over one million gallons. My
water rights on the Arun are only four
million gallons a year and anyhow the
ability of my pump to cover the trees

does not exceed three acres at a time. Water, therefore, for me is out.

Another method, which has never been properly used in this country, is large fans each standing twenty-five feet high, These, driven by electricity or diesel, drag the warm air from above down onto the trees. Frost comes from radiation of heat up into the sky. A flat piece of ground with no grass on it will not lose as much heat as a grass sward from every leaf of which warmth is radiated upwards and lost.

The method which for many years I and others used extensively was the burning of smudge pots. These were three gallon diesel stoves each with a chimney. We ourselves had four thousand of them. They were lit by flaming petrol being dropped onto the surface of the oil. We had three of these petrol droppers and I never really understood why they did not explode and kill us. They were made from two gallon petrol cans with a wick and a small tube. When tilted, the petrol dropped out from the tube, was ignited by the wick and fell flaming onto the diesel. The diesel burnt with a smoky flame and, when the smoke got up some thirty feet, it formed a layer of smog which cut off the radiation from the sky. There was also some heat thrown directly onto the trees by the stoves. Nowadays the burning of four thousand dirty fires to create a heavy smog would hardly be popular.

In the days when diesel was, to the best of my memory, about three pence a gallon, we might burn approximately five thousand gallons a night and it made financial sense. The lighting of the pots was only one of the problems. Having placed the diesel pots on all the lowest parts of the orchard and filled them from a diesel tanker which I had had converted from Lloyd George's old sprayer, one then had to have an alarm system. This led by wire from the control position some four hundred yards away to my bedroom.

The alarm was set one degree above the temperature at which we intended to light the smudge pots. However strong the batteries were, the alarm bell gave only the lightest of tinkles as it lost its power over the long stretch of wire.

When waiting for the bell it was very difficult to sleep. One knew the frost was coming because of the combination of a clear sky and little moisture in the air. This I could measure with a special thermometer. At last the tinkle of the alarm bell would come, I would telephone my foreman and we would meet at the control position each carrying torches and matches for the petrol droppers. Then came a period of waiting under the starlit sky with the frost beginning to turn the leaves of the trees to silver, I have spent what seems like hundreds of hours pacing with my foreman from thermometer to thermometer. What a

Why wasn't my foreman
a beautiful girl?

waste of lovely nights. Why wasn't he a beautiful girl? Those nights however got my normally silent foreman to talk.

One of the extraordinary stories that he told me of his father's youth was of the raids by the hamlet of Toat on Bedham, Stopham, Kirdford and Wisborough Green, all a few miles away. It had been the custom for the men to gather about once in five years and to march across country at night to raid the other hamlets and to rape the girls. The attack had to be carefully planned and was a great event. It resulted in a return raid which was normally left for at least a year. I have never found any confirmation of this strange story but I am sure it is based on fact and, over a thousand years, was nature's way of avoiding interbreeding in an area where travel was very difficult because of the heavy clay.

One of the villages attacked in the far past had been Ebernoe.

"Don't ye go near a girl from Ebernoe," said Alfred to his sons, "their children all be dwarfs".

Later I read that Ebernoe, before the

village was wiped out by the plague, had specialised in the production of dwarfs. There were always 20 or 30 for sale at the annual fair at Ebernoe Common. Around the fifteenth century fortunes were made by exporting Ebernoe dwarfs to the courts of Spain and Russia. Unwanted children were taken in from all around and dwarfed by the use of the juice of knotgrass, the dwarf elder, and the daisy, all of which produce allelochemicals to stunt competing plants. The same chemicals evidently work on animals, Francis Rabelais produced an almanac in 1532 on how to use the plants to stunt children. In the Midsummer Nights' Dream Lysander says

"Get you gone, you dwarf
You minimus, of hindering knotgrass made."

Another of his tales was how, as a boy, he helped his father catch small birds for the pot. At night they would lay a double net, known as a batfowler, along the side of a quickthorn hedge. They would then beat the hedge, the birds would fly out and get entangled and there was the basis for sparrow pie, or rather songbird pie.

Year after year we walked the moonlit orchards together and Alfred told me a lot about Sussex.

"When a girl do say "do adone" she means you to go on but when she says "Adone-do" she means you to stop".

Before he said that, I had never thought of him as a young man wandering in the valley with a girl beneath the may trees and with the wild roses flowering pink and white in every hedgerow. "When we were young and easy, under the apple boughs we'd lie."

He had a belief in charms and old remedies.

"My chillun never had whooping cough bad, I gie em a roasted field mouse".

"For me rheumatics I carry a potato, must be stolen mind".

"My father did say that for ague (malaria, formerly very common in Sussex) roll a gurt spider in a cobweb and swallow it live."

Roll a gurt spider in a cobweb and swallow it.

"I never needs no dentist, I allus wear a pair of moles feet hung around me neck".

"If hearing be bad, hang an adder in the sun, When it do drop oil, put the oil in yur ear."

When the temperature dropped to the right degree at the lowest point we would start to light. We knocked off the lids of each pot, dropped in the lighted petrol and then on to the next pot. Four thousand pots take quite a lot of lighting. In order to save diesel we would light alternate pots in the hope that these would hold the frost. It sometimes did. On other nights the thermometers spaced all across the orchards would show a brief upswing when we lit and then down they would plunge again, until in the end every fire was ablaze. Our doctor, returning late at night from a call, remembers seeing the whole of our hill aflame. It was a lovely sight among the blossom.

When the frost broke through our defences I felt much as I did when the German army broke through behind us in 1940. It was a feeling of sick despair; all that effort wasted and how would the farm survive?

As the sky lightened and at last the great yellow sun came edging over Toat hill, we would continue the ceaseless patrol of the thermometers. This was the most dangerous moment and on some nights we would still be lighting one hour after dawn. At last the temperature would edge up and now one could see the frost on every leaf and bud. Had we or had we not held the temperature to that vital last degree? A flower is either killed or it lives. A tenth of a degree may make all the difference.

Now we had the job of putting out the lamps and this one did by slamming the lid hard on the funnel. Nine times out of ten this would work, but, after one had passed, some lamps would burst into flame again with a thump. Before the final lamp was extinguished the other staff had come on duty and at last one could go home to a bath and breakfast.

Several nights of frost left one's nerves on edge. One of our best girls remarked on the bad frost damage and asked if I'd seen it.

I did not bring the dreadful frost or jump about with glee I do my job and won't be druv so don't you shout at me.

175

"Of course I bloody have," I snarled at her.

Next day she handed me an envelope. In it was a short poem.

"I did not bring the horrid frost
Or jump about with glee
I do my job and mun be druv
So don't you shout at me."

I apologised and she is still with us many years later.

Now came the next chore. The two hundred gallon tanker moved slowly along the lines of pots and, when emptied, returned for refilling to the main tanks. We only had enough diesel on the farm for two nights, so early on we had to estimate the diesel we had used that night and order up a big tanker from the oil company. They gave us priority in delivery.

Frosts were supposed to finish on May 22nd, but one year we were badly frosted on May 25th and 26th and in 1961 on June 5th and 6th. This last was the latest frost ever recorded. That date is driven into my mind. We had

had a good year and we had taken David and Didi Archer to dine and dance at Quaglinos. When we came out at three in the morning I looked at the sky.

"By God," I said, "we have lost our crop." When we got back the apples, which were already 8 mm across, felt spongy. I prayed that they would recover but three days later those on the lower slopes dropped off.

The staff, while I was away, had been unable to do anything as we had already emptied and collected the oil pots. The small crop which we finally picked sold for very high prices. At first I refused to send my apples to market.

One of my most reliable wholesalers, Barry Collingridge, telephoned me.

"David, we are desperately short of apples. The price is £2 for 30 pounds, It's never been so high before, you'd better send us a load."

"Barry, when it's £4 a box, telephone me again."

"It'll never go so high. The retailers won't pay the price!"

"We need the money, the crop was desperately short, so please try for it."

England for a week was starved of apples and Barry telephoned me.

"It's there, £4 a box, can I sell today for delivery tomorrow?"

We graded the crop in a few days and it was all sold quickly. A crop of 5,200 boxes fetched us over £18,000.

6

Hailed Again and a Lion

APPLE growing at the end of the war had been fashionable. We had two military families near to us. General Maxse at Fittleworth had planted an excellent orchard which his son Major Maxse was now running. In the early days I used to go over there for advice. John Maxse was completely dominated by his father and although the general was now bedridden his wishes were still law. On a farm walk an expert gave John some sound advice.

"I can't do that," said Major Maxse, who was aged over sixty. "My father wouldn't let me".

I enjoyed my visits to his house in Fittleworth but I was normally asked to go over early so that by 12.30, having walked the small and immaculate farm, we could settle down between the two of us to polish off at least a bottle of his excellent sherry. I used to drive home in a daze and go to sleep.

General Renton, five miles in the other direction, had hit the peach disaster. At his club in the 1950's peaches were considered to be the fruit of the future. A member had planted an acre and when they first cropped had sold them at the staggering price in those days of 8/- per pound. With that wonderful crop he netted on one acre fifteen times the value of the land. The news spread: members and their friends imported peach trees by the thousand and many of them planted up five or ten acres. These never cropped. For years the barren trees could be seen in the orchards of many great landowners.

Callum Renton had Prince Feisal of Iraq to stay with him each holiday. Feisal was then a schoolboy in his teens and was treated by the General as a Prince only on his arrival. After that he was treated as a schoolboy. Feisal's murder was a tragedy for the world.

Whenever one dined there on a summer night Callum would take the men out of the french windows into the garden 'to see France' and there we would stand in line peeing into the roses. He had a mild method of expressing his disapproval of anyone he disliked. "Not someone to have to stay for a week in the hols."

Another apple grower nearby was Prince Tomislav of Yugoslavia, a dark lively man of great charm. At one time I shared a secretary with him. She used to take Tomislav's children to tea parties at Buckingham Palace.

During apple picking an advisor came from Tomislav's farm to mine and found me in the orchards.

"Where do you people get your apple pickers?" he asked. "The last picker I talked to was a King. The King of Yugoslavia."

★ ★ ★

In 1961 the crop was so small that we were able to get away in early October for Paula's cousin's wedding in France.

We were on the way to the Southampton ferry when I realised I had forgotten my top hat. We were passing Petersfield where David Archer farmed; he was away, but I had worked there and knew where the house key was. I also remembered that he kept the hat on the top of the wardrobe in the spare room. We were behind time, but to Paula's fury I detoured. The hat was not where I remembered. As the minutes ticked away I searched the house. At last I found the hat and raced back to the car. We caught the night ferry by a whisker. Throughout our marriage Paula has always been early for everything and has seen to it that I have never actually missed a train or plane.

It was a good thing I had the top hat because the wedding was full of uniforms and the reception was at the bride's family's chateau. Few of the French aristocracy, in those days anyhow, spoke such an uncivilised language as English. During the five hour lunch my schoolboy French flowed as fast as the wines. The main course was a giant fish, was it really five foot long? Carried in by four men it was marched round the room to great applause. It turned out to be, of all things, a pike.

I had been asked by our cousin not to

Carried in by four men it was marched
round the room to great applause

call myself a farmer, but a landowner.

An Admiral in full uniform came up
to me.

"I hear you have some land near
Hampshire."

"Yes, some hectares."

"I knew a Hampshire landowner, he
was in the Navy during the war, a tall
man, lives near Romsey. Had some sort
of job in the Far East. Have you met
him?"

"Perhaps you mean Mountbatten."

"Ah yes, that's the name."

"I can't say I know him well." I said trying to keep my end up.

Paula's English fairness won the heart of the father of the bride, a cavalry Colonel who looked like but hated de Gaulle. Without us knowing he packed our car with wine from his own vineyard. We blithely went through the customs, fortunately unchecked.

★ ★ ★

Apples have always been subject to political pressures. From the safe haven of their jobs in the European capitals, civil servants have over the years thought up many disastrous plans for apples. What follows is accurate in outline but not in detail.

After the war in 1946 when Italy was in a very bad way, in the Ministry of Agriculture in London some conversation such as this occurred.

"We can get them to grow apples. The Northern plains would be excellent for apple growing. We can give them a market here in England".

So off went a Ministry of Agriculture team to teach the Italians how to grow apples. Large subsidies were supplied by the Americans and thousands of acres of fruit farms were laid out.

A couple of years passed and the Dutch lost their East Indies.

"We've got to bring them back here," said some Dutch official, "What can we do that will use their skills and take them off our backs?"

"I know", said another, "they can grow apples on the new polders".

Fifteen thousand returning colonials were allocated approximately ten acres each and given subsidies. The soil was excellent and to show them what to do they drew heavily and for free on the expertise of our East Malling Research Station.

A few more years passed. France lost the war in Algeria. "We have got to bring them all back here. What can we do to give them a living and take them off our backs?"

"I know," said a civil servant, "we will give them each ten acres and they can grow apples and peaches".

"But there is no good irrigated land available".

"We will put them on the best soil on the plateau above Avignon, It only needs irrigation and it will grow anything, There's spare water in the Rhone".

The French Government borrowed the money from the American Government on the condition that American irrigation equipment was used. Fifteen thousand growers were moved in, and each was given approximately ten acres.

The Americans put in great pumping stations on the Rhone. A vast scheme costing many millions of pounds was laid out on the land allocated.

So what happened? When the Dutch growers' trees came to fruition they ruined many Italian growers. Then the French trees came into bearing, Some fifty per cent of the Dutch farms went out of production. It didn't end there. When all the orchards in France were in full bearing twelve thousand out of the fifteen thousand Dutch growers granted land and subsidies, went out of business. This left three thousand very efficient growers who are still there. The French continued to expand and when they got on to the Golden Delicious they had a winner. This is when they began to bankrupt the English grower. Their advertising of "le crunch" was brilliant.

When I started apple growing there were three thousand reasonably successful English apple growers. Indeed, at one moment almost every great estate, including the Queen's at Sandringham, had its commercial apple orchard.

Through the intervention of the three governments gross over-production of apples was engendered. For the last fifteen years there has been an apple mountain in Europe. The French action also created a peach surplus and many of their own established growers of white peaches have been forced out by the cheaper yellow peach which has nowhere near the flavour of the older varieties but travels better.

Foreign growers vary greatly in their reception of visitors. South African Boers dress up to the nines and feed you very generously; the orchards are ignored. English South Africans show you their orchards and afterwards give you very strong drinks. The Dutch show their orchards and hurry you off the farm without food or drink, They are eager to get back to work, All growers across the world have one thing in common, they welcome other growers and willingly exchange information.

★ ★ ★

As growing has become more technical, advice has become essential. The problem is what advice to accept. Advisors are inclined to be temperamental and sensitive. After Basil Furneaux died my next advisor, Peter Hamer, was energetic but I could not bring him indoors because he shouted and his voice boomed through the house. He was however good at getting other advisors down for special problems.

I was having trouble with docks and he arranged for a free visit from the main weed expert in England. This little man arrived, looked at the sky, saw it was going to rain and wearing a little bobble hat and an anxious expression, hurried out into the orchard. He looked at my docks in horror.

"These are going to spread like wildfire," he said. "They will soon be all over the farm. You must dig them out at once. Put all your men on to it".

The main weed expert in England

"But," I replied, "my men are on other work, spraying, grass cutting. We are very busy".

"Leave all that," he said. "Get them all out here digging with those long dock forks, the soil moisture level is just right".

As the first drops of rain fell he hurried back into the house, exhausted by his 400 yard walk.

"Docks," he confided to me, "are terrible things, I hate them, it is the duty of all of us to eradicate them".

Next day I had five men digging docks. They dug for five days and by then we had cleared one acre. There were 60 acres of orchard to go. I stopped the work and have never dug another dock out of grass. It was another insight on how narrow a view experts may take. There is no surer way of going bankrupt than to put into practice all the advice one receives; the problem is how to be selective.

Some years later I experimented with growing docks in order to aerate the soil. There was a patch of stunted trees growing in heavy clay in one corner of Eight Acres orchard; I sowed dock seed there. The docks grew three feet high and when they finally died each root left a long thin hole. Because the water was now able to get away easily through the holes made by the docks the trees then began to flourish. I was lucky however to avoid the apple disease of dock sawfly which can be devastating. There are two main types of docks. The bloody-veined dock, which has a narrower leaf and a different seed, is regarded as a delicacy by bullfinches.

The success of a farm depends upon the wellbeing of its worms. There is one fungicide which is fatal to them but is good in suppressing canker. It is widely used elsewhere in the world but in England we now steer clear of it. Once after spraying this material the ground became slippery with dead worms. When I saw this I knew I had committed a crime against nature.

The success of a farm depends
on the well being of it's worms

Worms open up the soil to air and water and in doing so drag leaves and small pieces of wood deep down. Fallen leaves carry last year's fungus diseases but by the spring in a Cox orchard all the leaves, if you have plenty of worms, have disappeared. They have been pulled down into the soil. In a Bramley orchard this is not so and about a third of the leaves remain on the surface. It was not until a few years ago that the scientists realised that this is because the normal population of worms is able to pull down (say) twenty million leaves per acre, which is the amount a Cox orchard produces, but the Bramley has (say) thirty million leaves an acre and so ten million are left on the surface. If you walk across healthy soil in the winter you will see little piles of debris. This is where the worms have been out during the night collecting the leaves and sticks but have not yet pulled them down into the soil, They can move debris some eight feet across the orchard floor.

★ ★ ★

The next two years were good. When a farm has been starved of finance and the money flows in, it runs like water into parched land and vanishes just as fast. We bought two new tractors, a new spraying machine, a new mower, all the cottages were repainted, the gates repaired, the ditches were dug deep and the long farm drive was heavily retarred.

We bought another twenty acres, built a cottage, and planted four thousand young trees. The men with their bonuses bought cars, television sets and washing machines. I said to Paula "Let's have a really long holiday skiing in Switzerland".

"No," she replied, "We'll go up the Nile".

And so we did.

She had never before been out of Europe. Egypt, with its dirt, poverty and ancient history, epitomises everything of the East. We were there before the days of mass tourism, and we saw Abu Simbel in its original position. The captain of the boat had a sense of drama; when we were all dining the ship turned into the beach and he switched on the floodlight illuminating the gigantic figures of the temple.

Next year continued the upswing. We built two more cottages, bought a Land Rover and another tractor and put in more drainage.

★ ★ ★

In 1964 we had our second and very strange hailstorm. On May 30th we saw a dreadful black cloud advancing directly on us. From its centre lightning flashed. Paula and I collected the children and the two dogs and all huddled together on our large double bed. It had a wooden frame and so seemed the safest place, A whirlwind struck our conical hill and our hill only. It didn't hit anywhere else. The wind that swirled around was full of sharp and brittle hailstones. They had little weight but for ten minutes they pounded the hill from every angle, up and down and sideways. As we lay there with the hail rattling on the windows from the south, the east, and the north, there was a blinding lightning flash into our room and onto the frost alarm bell. This was hurled across the room and the radiator was scorched black. When the storm cleared each tiny apple measuring under five millimetres in diameter had been struck some dozen times from all sides and even from below; the hail was piled up along the french windows.

We had insured heavily for hail, but the cover did not start until June 1st, as that was thought to be the first day apples could be damaged. We were therefore uninsured.

Hail makes men go grey with shock and after a bad hailstorm the fruit world becomes silent. Like hurt animals crawling into a den no one wishes to speak about it, there are no interfarm telephone calls.

This hailstorm had an extraordinary effect. Normally hail dents an apple and if it cuts the skin the cut heals with heavy russet and later the apples tend to split at that mark. This time the apples were very small and every strike resulted in a bump. As the apples grew the bumps were at first remarkably ugly, but surprisingly no splits followed. In August as the skin stretched the first layer of heavy russet was dropped off. The bumps remained however and after considerable thought I decided to market all the apples as grade II to cover me with the new E.E.C. regulations, but, ignoring the bumps, labelled them also with the recently discontinued English grade names of Fancy, which used to be first class and Choice, which used to be second class. I overstamped all the labels "hail". In each box we put a little slip which read:

"These apples are sound, but damaged by hail.
Children love the little bumps."

It worked well; we set our price five per cent below the market price and the apples cleared quickly. The phrase "children love the little bumps" was regarded to my surprise as a dirty joke in the market, and made our name memorable. For some years we had requests for apples with the little bumps.

When an apple tree is hailed heavily the tree stops growing and puts all its energy into sealing the frayed edges of the leaves. For about ten days the apples too stand still: this loss of size is never made up, and may amount to about five millimetres in the diameter of every apple. It is a fact that loss assessors find difficult to understand.

★ ★ ★

Much later, in 1980, I insured as usual in early March against frost and hail. If you cover fifty per cent of the average of your last four crops the charge is about four per cent of the sum insured. I very rarely claim, but, when the clear night skies of April and May threaten the future of all of us, it takes a great load off one's mind to know that fifty per cent of the money will be coming in.

When the danger of frost is over, which is regarded as May 31st, one has the option of increasing one's insurance for hail from fifty per cent up to ninety per cent at a premium of six per cent of the balance. One cannot do this if one has already reported frost damage. In 1980 the insurer, one we were using for the first time, telephoned me.

"You're very underinsured, Mr Atkins. We can increase you up to ninety per cent of your average crop if you wish?"

"No thank you, it's too expensive."

"Because of your good record, I can give you a special discount of twenty per cent."

"I'll think about it." This was on a Wednesday.

On Thursday I telephoned to take up the extra insurance, and on Friday morning posted the confirmatory letter.

On Monday we went on holiday down to the Dart. As we drove westward we passed through terrible hail. It was no ordinary storm; the banked clouds stretched heavy and menacing from one horizon to the other.

"I'm sure we've been hailed," I said to Paula.

That evening I telephoned my manager.

"Have we been hailed?" I asked.

"The other farm is ruined, but Tullens is alright. The storm passed one mile to the south of us."

"Do you know the insurer's telephone number?"

"Yes, I have already claimed an estimated £60,000," he replied.

To get the money we had to pick and sell every battered apple. The cost of getting them in was nine thousand pounds and the yield from their sale was eight thousand nine hundred pounds, so that added one hundred pounds to the claim.

The insurer's agent, a very odd man, kept on ringing me up throughout the sale of the crop.

"If you put the apples in woven baskets with handles and decorate the baskets with ribbons the public will pay more."

"Retailers aren't stupid," I replied

"They'll soon see that these apples are third grade or worse."

The crop was insured with Lloyds so we got our money; it turned out to be close to the Manager's estimate.

★ ★ ★

1964

The first vet we used for our cattle and turkeys was Morris. His wife had been at school with Alfred, who had had a soft spot for her as a girl. During the frost nights as we walked together I had from him the running story of the fierce upsets of that marriage. When Morris tried and failed to murder his wife's lover with a humane animal killer the consequent trial caught the front pages of the world's press — "The humane murderer".

Later, when his wife finally left him, Morris developed a grudge against people in general. He bought himself a lion and erected a cage about ten yards from the road. The lonely lion roared at night, which disturbed the neighbours. Their children however were fascinated and would creep up to the cage and try and feed the animal.

As a county councillor I was asked to go and see him. As usual he was well dressed, wearing a bow tie and had a jaunty air about him.

He was wearing a bow tie and had a jaunty air about him.

"I'm sure you realise how upset your neighbours are by your lion. You don't want that do you?"

"I certainly do, my neighbours have been upsetting me for years. Everything I do they are on the blower to someone.

You know what the bastards have done about my cattle?"

"No, I only know about the lion."

"The bloody neighbours have got me struck off for starving my cows. I tell you what, squire, I love my cows and I hate my neighbours, all of them."

"But their children might get hurt."

"If I had my way they would all get eaten, the noisy little buggers."

The District Council tried twice to stop him keeping the lion, but failed, and when to everyone's relief it died he at once bought a leopard.

It was most upsetting to see these intelligent big cats kept in such lonely misery. All day they paced endlessly up and down the small cage. There is or was no law which could get him. The law usually proves useless except to the very poor and the very rich.

When Morris was struck off for the second and final time he proceeded to make a rich living by buying diseased cattle at markets. With his uncanny power to cure them, he soon had a second Rolls Royce and a steady stream of changing girlfriends of all colours. Where in the world did he find them?

To the end of his life he continued to annoy his neighbours in every possible way. He left derelict vans on the roadside and he herded his cattle onto the old bridge in Pulborough where they dunged heavily on the village footpath, It was a foolish thing to do. People get very upset about footpaths and in fact the West Sussex County Council gets more letters yearly about footpaths than about children's education. The Ramblers Association is the strongest and most subtle pressure group in the countryside.

* * *

The destruction of prunings is a difficult and used to be a back breaking job. For many years we put all the canker in fertilizer bags to be carried in and burnt on our drawing room fire. The other prunings we put in piles, either to be burnt on a moving steel sledge fire, or collected in trailers to be taken to big bonfires.

When silage came into fashion and whirling flails were used to cut the grass, some of us realised that we could mash our prunings using the same type of machine but with heavier blades. The new machine was made to our specification and I had a demonstration on my farm.

"How ridiculous," said David Archer, "It'll spread disease and canker all over the farm."

Anyhow I bought one, and am now on my second. It used to be a dangerous machine in that the force of the flails threw the wood chips both forwards and backwards at great speed. This is now avoided by rubber curtains, both at front and back, but as a secondary precaution the staff wear helmets.

The machine chops the wood into splinters of one inch to twelve inches in length. These lie on the ground and there the worms and the other processes of nature gradually destroy them together with the canker spores. The wood gives back to the soil all the goodness and trace elements which we used to burn, and in the early spring rains the carpet of chips helps support the tractor wheels. It does however give one a great many punctures.

When I remember that we used to carry every pruning to a bonfire and the great deal of physical effort that this took, I much regret that the flail chopper did not come in earlier.

★ ★ ★

The first picking camp had taught us a great deal. For the next big crop we got the campers in late on Sunday evening so they could not get bored. They worked well and each evening they walked up through the wood to drink at the Rose and Crown.

There was a tough gang in the county and the news soon spread that there were new girls about. The leather jacketed motor cyclists gathered. The girls stopped going to the pub, but the gang came up to the camp, and for some nights virtually took it over.

The men in the camp that year were not at all tough. The leader of the gang ordered them to stay in the caravans while all the girls were ordered out to sit around the camp fire. Amazingly they all obeyed. For two nights the girls were molested and harassed. In the end one of them, coming up for a bath, knocked timidly at our door.

"There's a gang of motor cyclists in the camp," she said. We could hardly believe our ears.

"Tell them to go away".
"They look dangerous. I'm frightened".

"Go on down David," said Paula, "and turn them out".

"Me?", I said, "what are the men in the camp doing?".

"They are all hiding in the caravans," replied the girl. While Paula took up a truncheon and set off to confront the invaders, I hurried to the telephone to get the police. In the dark Paula fell into a ditch and so, fortunately, did not get to the camp.

The gang leader was greatly feared in the neighbourhood. He had run down and killed another man by accident after a party. The gang could not resist gunning their motorcycles and, warned by the roar of their arrival, I would leap to the telephone and ring the police. We had been told by the police not to confront them, and at first I agreed with the advice.

When however in spite of nightly visits from the police the motorcyclists continued to come, I spoke to my staff.

"They arrive every night at about 10.30 p.m. We'll all go out together and order them away".

"Order them away?" exclaimed my new charge hand in horror.

"Yes, it should be quite easy".

"Quite easy?"

"Yes, quite easy and the police will be up shortly afterwards".

"I was at school with that man," said my charge hand. "I never wish to meet him again."

The gang continued to come up and it was not until the end of the camp that I discovered that one of the girls in the caravans had fallen in love with the gang leader. When the camp finished she did not go back to Hamburg University but moved in with him.

★ ★ ★

1965

Body odour in the pack house used to be a problem which has now disappeared. We had one energetic young man who looked clean but who smelt terrible.

"You're the foreman, Alfred," I said, "go and tell Gary that he must bath more frequently."

Alfred, as was usual when he didn't like my orders, went silent. Although quick to criticize the faults of staff, as any good foreman should be, he clearly felt that this was beyond the call of duty. The situation continued for some days with both of us chickening out. I then had an idea. I moved a local woman well known for her quick tongue into the pack house. She arrived, sniffed around, and within a few minutes had located the smell.

She did not mince her words. "You smell horrible Gary, you have a bath tonight or we'll all walk out". It worked.

When Gary and his wife finally left we got into the cottage. The lavatory, including the walls, was absolutely foul. Before we could put anyone else in Paula, with the help of a good tempered au pair girl, nobly washed down every wall.

★ ★ ★

The smells in the orchard are a constant source of pleasure and interest. The fox smell hits one whenever one crosses its tracks, but the subtler smells are rain after drought, cut grass, newly ploughed land, ripe strawberries in the sun, ripe apples, the fungus smell of autumn and the smoke of bonfires.

Each apple variety has a different scent which must be very clear to the bees. At one moment they won't touch Worcesters which although in bloom evidently have no smell. As these are the main pollinators for Cox, one looks on in despair at the bees busy in the Cox but doing absolutely no good because they are not carrying any Worcester pollen. Then next day you may see that the bees are on both types of tree and pollinating each flower they touch; the Worcester scent has come. James Grieve and Lord Lambourne both have a faint and distinguishable smell and are excellent pollinators. They flower for long periods every year, both opening before Cox comes into bloom and always outlasting it. James Grieve is ready for cooking just before Bramley and at that time is a large green apple. Later on it colours up and becomes a delicious eating apple. Because it bruises very easily indeed, it can only be picked by experts and can certainly never go over a grader. We pick down to 65 mm diameter, direct into the blue lined wooden boxes in which they are sold.

7

Marketing, Cold Stores and Campers

1965

ONE of my Surrey fruit growing friends, call him Richard, had green fingers and was excellent at budding and grafting. In his large house he had benches laid out below the curving staircase in the great hall, and he spent his evenings making trees, He could not bear to waste these, and so each year he planted some ten acres. His planting consisted of crisscrossing the ground with a sub-soiler and at each junction a girl casually thrust in a tree. It looked ridiculous, but the trees grew.

He came to see me for financial advice. "What shall I do?" he asked. "The bank is being extremely rough with me."

He rented his farm and an examination of his balance sheet showed that he had hardly any assets and an overdraft of over £30,000.

"The bank can't do anything but support you," I replied, "They must go on lending to you if they are not to lose all their money."

The following week, Richard, to the horror of his bank manager, bought an elderly but expensive Bentley. In this four of us went on a fruit tour of the Midlands. He drove as casually as he farmed.

From the back I called on him to slow down, Richard, as people so often do if you criticize their driving, went faster.

The crash when it came only caved in the front of the Bentley but the other small car was badly crushed. No one was hurt.

"The bank manager won't like this," said Richard disconsolately as he eyed the wreck. "I'm not comprehensively insured."

He went on his headlong course to ruin. His trees flourished and his crop increased, but he had no cold stores, so much of his fruit went bad. The money that did flow in, he didn't bank but kept hidden around the house and under his mattress. The inevitable happened: much of it was stolen.

He kept the money hidden under his mattress

The bank became crosser, and he fell behind with his rent.

He approached the next crop, ordered two hundred tons of top quality cold storage and built a tarmac road through the farm. All this was done on credit. By now most of his cheques were bouncing but his farm looked so prosperous that people accepted his orders. He used to ask me over frequently. On one occasion he remarked.

"Do you think those trees are all right David?"

"No, they are far too close, next winter you might consider taking half of them out."

"No time like the present. George," he called, "Get a tractor and pull out every second tree". This was the sort of decision I myself agonized over for months.

When the next crop came he was not there. He had gone off to Australia to watch the Test series.

When he came back his landlord had foreclosed and he was out. He was a good grower and a nice man, but had no sense of priority. He threw away a really good business; a sensible wife might have saved him.

A bankruptcy sale of any fruit farm is particularly heart rending when there are children watching their ponies, bicycles and even their rocking horse going under the hammer, I shall never forget the first one I went to. All the family had left afterwards was a caravan and a puppy.

215

★ ★ ★

One couple we had on the farm took me in for some months. Tall and lithe he strode about always looking busy.

"I can't abear that chap," said Alfred. "He be a fire-spannel."

"What's a fire-spannel?" I asked.

"You'd call it a lazy so and so," he replied.

Picking and pruning are great revealers of real worth because one can measure the production. At the picking season I checked the apples as usual.

"I'm afraid you're bruising, Mrs Brown," I said. "Please be more careful".

"Of course sir, I'm terribly sorry sir, it won't occur again sir."

Later in the day I went down to check her apples again. As I approached through the trees I heard her say to her husband.

"Me bruising, I gave him a right talking to I can tell you. You can take your bloody apples, I said, and stick them right up your . . . That's what I told him."

"Quite right," said her husband, "We

mun be druv, I allus has a bit of a sit down and smoke at the farm bottom when he be out of sight."

Alfred was right and I had them both out after harvest.

★ ★ ★

Cruelty in the camp now seems to have vanished but early on we had some astonishing examples of it. One rather spinsterish girl, a good worker, used to go to bed each evening at 9 o'clock. She believed that she needed not less than ten hours of sleep a night. Two men took against her. They would sit by the camp fire drinking beer and with a pile of apples (damaged ones I hope) beside them. Every twenty minutes one of them would hurl an apple at the aluminium side of the caravan inside which the poor girl was desperately trying to get to sleep. Imagine her lying there waiting for the next thunderous crash. Her health broke down and she left. As I drove her down to the station she told me what had happened.

Then there was the doctor's son who

was in a caravan with a male nurse. He was not able to stand up for himself and the male nurse, who should have known better, baited him unmercifully, He collapsed and Paula was called down to see him. She rang his father.

"I think you should come over at once and collect your son".

"What's wrong with him?"

"He's in a deep depression. I think it needs taking seriously".

"Oh you know these lads — it's probably just a bad hangover".

But it wasn't, he had been tipped over into schizophrenia. It was a terrible blow for the family.

★ ★ ★

When I first came into farming there was far more social awareness of jobs than there is now. Potato picking was

Potato picking was the lowest job

the lowest and the dirtiest job. Then there was strawberry picking and higher than both of these but still not then fully acceptable was apple picking. Nowadays this differentiation has gone. Apple picking is now largely done by the middle classes and all picking is socially acceptable. This is not so yet in France and America.

In the States apple picking is social death and they can get few Americans, black or white, to do it. The system there used to work in two ways. On the West Coast as the fruit ripened Mexicans under tough gang masters moved up from the south to the north following the harvests. The pickers were rigorously controlled and paid far less per hour than our English pickers. The grower, apart from checking quality, had little contact with them. It was much the system described in "The Grapes of Wrath".

On the East coast they flew in blacks from the Caribbean. These were kept under close guard and were not allowed into the towns. None of the local blacks from nearby, e.g. Washington and Baltimore, would turn their hand to what they regarded as demeaning slave type work. If one grew apples in Virginia I think one could start a social revolution there and soon have the middle classes picking fruit. Once they started people would enjoy the work and would tell their friends.

Apple growing in Virginia in the early 1980s was a mess. Large landowners had big neglected trees. They had been comfortable for too long and were at least ten years behind England. Since then, particularly on the West Coast, they have begun to catch up.

My advisor, Eric Gunn, was invited over to show them our pruning methods. With a large audience he was asked to demonstrate on some typical Virginian trees. He took a chain saw and cut six foot off the top of each tree. The audience gasped as each top came tumbling down.

"That's all you can do this year," he said. "I've let in light and air and the apples will be easier to pick."

★ ★ ★

Pickers come in all sorts. One little man who had worked for me for several years was well over seventy but he climbed to the top of his ladder and cleared the tallest trees. I had the impression that he had been in a clerical job all his life and, surprised at his agility, I stopped to talk with him.

"Tell me, Mr Wells, what did you do before you retired?"

"I was an entomologist, ever heard of Kingdon-Ward?" he asked, referring to a famous naturalist whom my family had known slightly in India. "He and I travelled the foothills of the Himalayas, and the mountains in Burma and China. While Kingdon-Ward collected plants, I collected insects".

"How did you travel" I asked.

"Usually on foot with twenty or thirty porters but sometimes we used mules".

I knew he was talking of a dangerous area where head hunting flourished.

When I wrote a book on the Burma war Mrs Kingdon-Ward came to see me. Her husband's books gave me a new view on how the plant kingdom works. Plants are territorial invaders. The reason we in England have relatively few types of plants compared with the Far East is that our plants marched south to avoid the ice age, and then had to fight their way back north when the temperature changed. This left outposts of northern plants on all the mountain slopes in Asia, so there they have the plants of both hemispheres and most of our garden flowers come from there.

* * *

In the 1960s the standard lay-out of an orchard was eighteen feet square which gives one hundred and thirty-four trees to the acre. Every fourth lane was a picking lane down which the tractors worked and on each side of which pickers had cants of eight trees each. Each picker was given a number which was repeated on his ladder, on his picking bucket and on the tickets with which he marked each box. We numbered the ladders because it helped pickers find their place each morning and also stopped the clever ones, when moved, from pinching a ladder nearer their new position, instead of carrying their own across the orchard.

Supervisors mapped out each orchard and could tell you at any time where each person was supposed to be. Most of the pickers were co-operative but some, and these were often the quickest pickers, would plot to get the best positions and would move themselves only when the supervisor was absent.

Young people are usually slower pickers than the middle aged housewife and, unless closely supervised, tend to be more casual about bruising. If however a youngster is good then he can be very good indeed. In my memory one stands out. She was a German au pair girl who worked in our house, but who used her time off to pick apples. Slim and tall her hands seemed to sweep across the branches and she had an output of over a hundred boxes a day when the average was about twenty-five. She never bruised. Good pickers thoroughly enjoy the work and will go on from dawn till dusk.

★ ★ ★

There has always been a great gap between what the grower gets for his apples and what the public pays. It was then about 50 per cent and now it is even more. It was worst in Covent Garden which in those days acted as a primary wholesaler; that is they tended to sell in big lots to secondary wholesalers who, over an area of about one hundred square miles, resold either to smaller wholesalers or to retail shops. Each layer of sales took another slice out of my pocket.

To combat this I travelled up through England and found big retailers who were selling direct to the public in the local market places. In my third year I packed the apples of my small crop into thin wooden boxes with nailed wooden lids. Off the lorries trundled around England dropping thirty or forty boxes at each place. These retailers took about a twenty-five per cent mark up; what they bought for a shilling they sold at 1/3d. What I had not fully grasped was that I was selling to the cheapest retailers in England. While they were selling a pound for 1/3d the retail shop round the corner, open all week and paying rates, was selling the same apples for about 1/6d. Their customers were not so cost conscious and their extra margin meant that they could buy at a higher price when they went to local wholesale markets.

In one of my journeys up north I could not find a room in Derby. I asked a policeman who advised:

"You might find a room in the Eagle Hotel".

I booked in there and while having a drink in the bar was told of a murder that had taken place in the hotel a few weeks before. It had been particularly unpleasant with blood splattered all across the walls.

"Do you remember which room it was?" I asked.

"Yes, it was number eight".

"That's all right," I replied, "I am in number twelve".

I went up to bed. In the middle of the night I woke up with a feeling of dread. The smell of new paint was oppressive. I lay in bed nervous and tense, a thought had struck me. I went out on to the landing. The rooms on the second floor ran from 7 to 13. I was in 12. I went up to the third floor and there the numbers ran in the reverse order to the numbers on my floor, I came back and looked carefully along the corridor. All the numbers had been reversed and I was sleeping in the original number 8 which was now 12.

* * *

For the next three years as our crop expanded rapidly I visited all the markets in the Midlands and as far up as Manchester. To do this one had to get up very early; the markets opened at five and closed at about half past nine. The best time to be there was about seven o'clock. Before choosing a wholesaler I would stand in the market and watch them selling. I opened up friendly relationships with wholesalers in markets in Southampton, Plymouth, Bristol, Cardiff, Liverpool, Manchester, Leicester, Derby, Nottingham and Covent Garden. Instead of giving actual results poor wholesalers have a habit of averaging prices. This is not only fraudulent but it also works to a growers disadvantage. On a dropping market the first 50 boxes may sell at £6.00 each and the last, a fortnight later, at £4.80. By keeping a daily record of all sales reported to me over the telephone, one soon learnt the truth. Liars do not have good memories and I found a fraud rate of about 8%, which meant changing one wholesaler a year. Some firms never cheated and I stayed with them for years.

It was a Manchester lorry at Tullens which the driver moved before roping down. As he drove forward five tons of apples tilted slowly outwards and fell in a welter of broken boxes and shattered fruit. I was away and Paula was called down and supervised the clearing up. The men were quite incapable of coping with the situation and indeed Alfred had disappeared to have his mid morning lunch. Nowadays our staff would cope.

Glasgow and Edinburgh were beyond the reach of my hired lorries but both cities have a reputation for eating very little fruit and vegetables. Scots in those days tended to have bad teeth and they could not bite into a Cox, but only into those soft red American apples which have no taste. Because of their poor diet Scots have a very high rate of heart disease.

Lorry drivers are usually helpful and very hard working. Getting the lorry to the right place at the right time was and is vital. Our despatches were planned to take account of the best market days and these varied across the country for each wholesaler. On these days the lorry had to get there in time for the start of the market at 5.00 a.m.

When the Government nationalised the transport industry it was a nightmare. If I wished to send up to Derby, a lorry came from the Government depot in Brighton, loaded up, went back to Brighton, spent the night there and did not deliver to Derby until two mornings later. It was expensive, slow and unreliable. After two years, to everyone's relief, all the lorries were sold off to private companies and nationalisation was scrapped.

I used to invite the wholesalers to come down and see the farm. When they did so I gave them lunch, and by this means I got to know their apple salesmen by their

Scots tended to have bad teeth

Christian names which, even then, were in universal use in markets.

I had only enough cold stores for 150 tons of apples while I was growing 700 to 1000 tons a year. I hired some more but none of our storage was capable of holding the fruit beyond Christmas so I had to sell fast.

Alan had copied a design for packing by which 30 lbs of apples, having been graded, could be slid into a box without bruising. This doubled our throughput and, working evenings and weekends, we reached a peak of seven thousand boxes a week graded, packed and despatched off the farm. This was over twelve ten ton loads which we sent to the twelve wholesalers on our list.

Few growers grade during Cox picking time and early each season we were able to fill the markets without much competition. Prices tend to sink all through October until they reach a low in early November by which time all those growers who have no cold storage should have cleared their crop.

Stored in a barn, Cox will only keep in really good condition to the end of October, In cold store at 38°F an apple will last until the middle of December. Then we come to 'gas' storage. The word gas alarms people but apples are alive and make their own. They breathe in oxygen and breathe out carbon dioxide. When this reaches five per cent of the atmosphere in the store one has to bring more air into the store as, if this is not done, the apple may be damaged internally by the carbon dioxide. This method will keep apples to the middle of January.

The next stage in storage is called 'scrubbed gas'. When the carbon dioxide in the store rises above five per cent, the air in the store is pulled by fan over paper bags of dehydrated lime. The lime extracts the excess carbon dioxide keeping it down to five per cent. Air is normally 22 per cent oxygen with 78 per cent nitrogen. Gradually the oxygen, which the apple turns to carbon dioxide by breathing, is reduced to two per cent, the carbon dioxide level being kept at 5 per cent, and the nitrogen rises to 93 per cent. This, which is quite difficult to do, will keep Cox in good condition at least to the end of February. The apple is in fact put into a deep sleep and, starved of oxygen, stops ripening.

The last stage, called low oxygen, is dangerous because if the oxygen level goes below a half per cent, the apple may suffocate and die. It depends therefore on very accurate instruments, an even spread of atmosphere across the store and constant monitoring. This is a stage

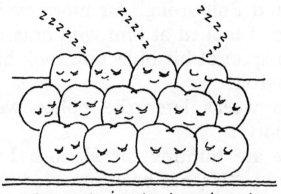

The apple is put into a deep sleep

I have not dared to try and is best left to specialists. Throughout all these methods only the natural breathing of the apple is used to adjust the gas levels.

Maddeningly the Golden Delicious stores extremely well and can easily be kept for a full year as can the Bramley. So far no one has been able to keep them in first class condition beyond a year. If they do, that will be the end of the small grower in England. When we had our next big crop I noted those in the camp who were at university. Two days before their terms started I took them off my payroll. One nice Scots boy objected strongly.

"Don't you want to go back to Edinburgh?" I asked.

"I find Pulborough far more exciting," he said. I looked at him with amazement and in spite of his objection took him off my payroll.

Two weeks later the police were at my door.

"We are hunting for Hamish Laing," they said. "He has been reported missing by his family".

"He's not here, he's gone back to university".

"The university doesn't know where he is," said the policeman. "I think there's a chance he's still in Pulborough."

"All right. I'll ask someone to see if they can find him".

It was reported back to me that Hamish was working as a bricklayer and was drinking regularly at The Five Bells. I told the police. They closed the case, he was no longer missing.

There was a pause of about three weeks and then a young voice came on the telephone:

"This is Hamish's mother. Could you tell me please — is Hamish still working in Pulborough?"

I said I would find out and telephone her back, which I duly did. He was still here.

Next week a friend of ours was travelling down on an almost empty train from London; opposite her was a very jittery girl. After one or two false starts she spoke.

"Do you by any chance live in Pulborough?" she asked.

"Yes," replied Caroline.

"Do you know the Atkins family?"

"Yes, I know them well".

"My fiance," said the girl, "has gone quite crazy. He has thrown up his course at Edinburgh and is working as a bricklayer in Pulborough. He was taking law and was going to be a solicitor".

I later heard that the girl had arrived like a little whirlwind at The Five Bells. She and Hamish had a stand up row but the barman and all the drinkers had come down heavily on her side.

"If you don't play fair by this young lady," said the barman, "I will see you never get a drink again in Pulborough". Hamish had gone off sheepishly. He later

wrote telling me that the University had taken him back and thanking me for my help.

★ ★ ★

Throughout our early camps we had eight 'students' to dinner each Saturday night. It was a pleasure to us but also helped to keep them on our side. A friend of my wife, who came down each year to help us on the accounting for the crop, was intrigued.

"Throughout the week," she remarked, "you treat them so toughly that they are all nervous of you, then on Saturday evening you ask them in and treat them as honoured guests. They love it but it throws them".

On one occasion the jersey which Paula had put into the Conservative jumble sale in the morning was back at our dinner table that same night. The campers were always the main buyers at that sale. They arrived in summer weather and then the cold winds of autumn swept in. After each sale the camp was transformed, riding breeches and boots, long woollen dresses, old fur coats and once a Locke hat which I coveted, all bought for a few shillings.

At the end of each camp we would give a drinks party; at it I would at last hear what had really been happening. One girl had booked in for two weeks but left after one. As I drove her to the station I asked her why she was leaving early.

"The men are no good," she said.

At the farewell party a Scots boy told

After each sale the camp was transformed

me of his first night in camp. The caravans were full and he had arrived bringing a small tent. He was exhausted with travelling, so he erected his tent, climbed into his sleeping bag and went straight to sleep.

"In the middle of the night," he said, "I was woken up. A naked girl was climbing into my sleeping bag".

"I have tried all the others," she whispered, "and they are no good". He did his best.

She was the only nymphomaniac that, to the best of my knowledge, we have ever had in the camp. The ungrateful men instead of welcoming her with open arms, made a joke of her.

That year we had an older man. John Cartland, who ran a language school for girls in Brighton, had booked in with three Swedish students but turned up without them — a great disappointment. John had been in the Navy during the war and had commanded a motor torpedo boat on raids behind the sandbanks on the German coast. However good he was at sea he could not find his way around our farm and frequently, to the intense annoyance of the supervisors, ended up picking apples in the wrong orchard.

Later we learned from the national

newspapers that, while caravanning in France, he had been murdered with an axe. Suspicion fell on his son but he was acquitted.

Another strange end was that of a friend in Norfolk who had gambled largely in potatoes. For a time he had great success in buying in thousand ton lots from Germany. Then it all went wrong and he owed over £200,000.

Thinking only of his wife he insured himself very heavily, arranged for a large dinner party, and had himself called away in the middle to deal with trespassers.

"I'll be back in half an hour," he said to his guests as he went out.

Taking his gun and dog he drove off to the far end of his farm, loaded his gun, put his dog's paw on the trigger and the gun to his head. He pressed the paw and killed himself.

The insurance company proved suicide and did not have to pay out. The dog, most unfairly, was put down.

The camp that year was a very large one. Local apple pickers were hard to get and we had to rely on campers. The bush telegraph of the young brought in many unsuitable applicants and we did our best to weed them out.

Two girls with beehive hairdos picked their way on their high heels through the mud giggling as they went.

"Brought your wellingtons?" I asked.

"Oh, do you pick in the rain?" they said. "We can't bear to get wet, it spoils our hair dos".

I let them stay for one night before putting them back on the train but they had the best of me. They each stole a blanket.

Another girl had written to me six months ahead from India booking a place. She arrived early one morning and I put her straight out to pick. The supervisor was soon on to me.

"That Shirley can't pick apples," she said.

"Why not?"

"Her hand misses them, she doesn't seem to see properly".

I moved her into the grading shed and gave her the easy job of putting liners into wooden boxes. She could not get them in straight. At twelve o'clock I gave her notice. At the lunch break I had a delegation of campers up to see me.

"We think you are being unfair to Shirley," they said.

"She can't work properly, why should I employ her?"

"You should be kind to her," said one girl, "she's on drugs".

"Come off it," I replied, "I'm not a rest home for drug addicts. If you want however she can work with you and you can draw joint wages on piece work". The girl rejected the idea.

As I took Shirley down to the station I asked her what she had been doing in India.

"I've been begging on railway stations," she said. "I made quite a good living at it. When they see I am white and helpless, even the poorest give".

"Is that all you do?" I said.

"Oh no," she said. "I make some money on the side, on the game, you know".

She must have been one of the first of the layabouts who were to flood into India over the next fifteen years.

Pruning is very complicated and
at first quite bewildering

8

Pick Your Own and the Manor Dispute

1965

WHEN grading you need a team of between eight to twelve people to man the machines. Many apple growers also produce raspberries and strawberries so that the staff used in doing so can later be employed in apple grading. It's a question of getting a balance of work throughout the year.

I started growing strawberries in 1965. We intended to send them to market and did so for two years. Then two big growers near me started a strong recruiting campaign for pickers, and bought buses to collect them direct from their homes. I was suddenly faced with a forty ton crop of strawberries and few pickers. The previous year at a game lodge in Kenya, I had met an American who had had a great success with a 'pick your own' strawberry farm on the East Coast. As we waited through the night for a leopard to take a bait he explained to me in a whisper how he did it. "Pick your own" was unknown in England at the time and I decided to try it.

I advertised, not very widely, and the public rushed in. Possibly because it was the beginning of the deepfreeze craze, the response was quite overwhelming. We had three people parking cars, two taking the money, one handing out baskets. The local road was so busy we had to make a one way system. For a few days the money poured in at a higher rate than we have ever taken it again.

Nowadays we perhaps recover our year's strawberry costs, but only just. In that extraordinary shortlived boom we covered one year's costs in three days.

Unfortunately the news spread; I saw two local growers creeping by in their Land Rovers. They were amazed to see cars coming in and out at three a minute and over one hundred in the car park.

I told everybody it was a failure; the pickers trampled on the strawberries, they ate as much as they picked, they wandered everywhere, but it was no good, next year there were ten "pick your own" farms near us. The following year there were one hundred across Sussex, and then it seemed in no time at all that they were everywhere. With the same speed that they started they are now dropping away in their hundreds. People don't freeze as many strawberries as they used to, also the imports of strawberries all the year round make them less of a treat.

Strawberries deteriorate the soil they use and it gets harder each planting to get a worthwhile crop. Raspberries last longer, but recently phytophera, a disease that kills the cane, has spread like wildfire across Scotland and England. Raspberries need cold weather in the winter and so they cannot be grown properly, thank heaven, in France or Italy. In the war I picked wild raspberries four thousand feet up in the Burma mountains.

Every year from June to September we take on two girls to help us. We have been extraordinarily lucky. Well mannered, clean and smiling, they have come from New Zealand, South Africa and Australia. Many of the customers have been abroad and can talk to them of their homelands. Some of our girls, with the help of their Embassies have gone to the Queen's Garden Parties.

There are two unexpected problems with "pick your own". Customers and our staff spend hours looking for lost car keys and wedding rings and also some pickers refuse to move to the end of the rows where the fruit is plentiful.

On the whole customers are pleasant, honest and patient, but sometimes we get a large family who all take small punnets and disappear for an hour into the field to eat. On one occasion we found a party behind a hedge with plates, sugar and cream eating our unpaid for raspberries.

Organised theft is relatively rare. Late

one evening after closing time our son Richard saw a man picking. He went across to him and as he did so, one after another, five men who had been lying flat between the rows, got up around him. They were using our trays to steal our fruit. In a fury he confiscated the strawberries. The danger of being beaten up never occurred to him.

On one occasion we had fifty picked boxes of apples stolen. I guessed the theft had been carried out by a family of rogues who were picking for me by day. Guarded by 5′ 4″ Alan I went down to sack them. Standing among a sea of unpicked apple trees I spoke to them.

"I'm sorry we are coming near the end of harvest, there is no more picking."

The five of them gathered around me, even the daughters topped me by four inches.

"But you took us on for two weeks."

"I miscalculated, you must finish up today."

I turned and walked away, my back feeling very vulnerable. To my relief they went quietly — they knew I knew.

Spud Rawlings was a man of great energy and charm. He did everything at top speed, and was one of the strongest men on the farm. He was as invaluable as he was unreliable. If he wanted one of my tools for use in his garden, it vanished.

"We're short of a spade and the draining rods, I expect you have had them Spud?"

"Come to think of it squire, I may have or yet again I may not." The tools reappeared.

Spud was in charge of strawberry picking where he was a great favourite with the girls of all ages. He was straight out of the Darling Buds of May.

"Come on Mrs. Gosling, get your pretty bottom moving. You're two trays behind". He loved the hot days with the girls in shorts and bikini tops kneeling between the rows, Some certainly were an intriguing sight. One bespectacled retailer would never just take his trays of strawberries and go. He would wander up to the pickers and chat, wiping his steaming glasses at intervals as he looked

249

at the row of kneeling girls.

Spud's wife watched him like a hawk. Certainly he stripped the pretty girls with his eyes, but probably through lack of opportunity not with his hands.

He ran me into a major row. Many fish and eel died in the small tributary which leads from the farm to the Arun, The water authority traced the pollution back to me. Spud, at knocking off time, had emptied a spray tank by running the lethal spray, one which we no longer use, into the ground near the stream. I was held to blame. On another occasion I found that, instead of saying that he'd been inaccurate in putting on fertilizer, he had emptied two surplus bags into the pond.

As I often quoted him Spud was famous in our house. When I was in local politics I regarded him as the voice of commonsense working class England. A voice which is largely ignored.

Spud says "the unemployment pay for the bloody layabouts is too bloody high".

Spud says "giving bloody single women with children a council flat is a bloody disgrace, encourages them to go out making babies" and he says "they get their bloody money out of my bloody pay". He rarely used "bloody" except to me in deference to my position as his boss; to everyone else he used the stronger word.

I inspected his cottage at intervals, picking my way between the pretty children who tumbled around.

"Spud," I said, "what is that dark brown liquid in those three lemonade bottles?"

"That, I dunno, I guess it's Gramoxone".

"Spud, one mouthful of Gramoxone, even if it is spat out at once, will kill a child."

"The kids are careful little buggers".

"And Spud, that is my Gramoxone, and in a lemonade bottle. I told you how dangerous it is."

"Well, you know how it is."

I did indeed know how it was, but all of us were fond of him.

* * *

As our trees grew we decided to train some local women to prune. Five of them joined us and at first I thought they would never learn. Every cut on an apple tree has a different result. A cut half way up a piece of first year (maiden) growth will stop that shoot from cropping for two years and will make it grow more strongly. A cut to a fruit bud will strengthen all the fruit bud on that lateral and also stop growth. Pruning is very complicated and at first quite bewildering. After four to five months the scales drop from some peoples eyes, they begin to understand what they are doing and prune with confidence. It is an art form which cannot be learnt properly in less than two seasons particularly as the condition and strength of the tree affects each decision. A good pruner is never bored. They are thinking of the effect which each cut will have on the tree in one, two or even three years time.

The best time to prune is when the sap is down in December to March. One moves very little in pruning and the problem of cold feet and hands becomes urgent. Gloves with fingers are not nearly as warm as mittens. Flexible waterproof mittens are not available in England and for many years I bought a supply of leather ski mitts from Switzerland. With the change of fashion skiers now are only able to buy gloves which are more expensive to make and not so warm. I am looking forward to fashion reverting to mittens when once again I can supply the farm with them. Cold feet also, particularly when you are standing in snow or frost, is a terrible problem. On very cold days the solution is to wear bedroom slippers inside galoshes. In England snow and frost tend to melt during the day so we cannot use the felt boots which are so successful in Russia.

★ ★ ★

In the early days when we were loading the cold store we filled each store seven boxes high, which was up to the level of the first stable type door. On the platform that we then had, one could walk on the corner posts of the boxes and, using roller conveyors, full boxes could be sent up to the stackers. Two people would stack,

on cold days the solution is to wear
bedroom slippers inside galoshes.

one would roll the boxes along, one
would stand on a platform and put the
boxes on to the roller conveyor and one
would pass the boxes on the trailer up
to the man on the platform. We used
to load twelve thousand boxes fourteen
high. Filled like this the store would take
a thousand more boxes than if it were
loaded by fork lift truck. With plenty
of energetic manpower available it was
quite cheap and, because of the sense of

achievement, quite fun.

The New Zealanders, the South Africans and the English working on the farm would rarely query the system. The Australians, however, would frequently point out that it would be easier with a fork lift truck.

"If I had a fork lift truck," I would reply, "I wouldn't need you".

To be fair to Australians, their frequent suggestions are sometimes useful, They have enquiring minds but usually are lazier than New Zealanders.

Australian girls from the East coast tend to be taller and stronger than those from the West but some of them cannot pick apples; their fingers are too strong and they bruise. If, however, an Eastern Australian is good she tends to be outstanding.

When one does mechanise it is not always productive. Now we have fork lift trucks and pallet trucks I sometimes see three men standing around waiting for the fork lift truck to move, say, twenty boxes. These could be moved by ordinary muscle power in a few moments but they wait for the machine and then all watch

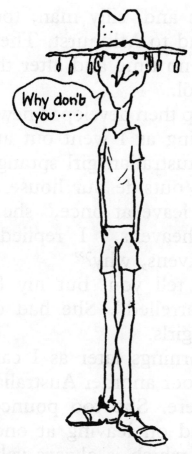

Why don'b you·····

Their frequent suggestions
are sometimes useful

it do the simple job.

After the problems of the first three camps we decided for the next camp to appoint a commandant. We found an ex-white hunter from Kenya. At first he maintained a good humoured and strict control, but then he fell in love with one of the girls and, silly man, took her for the weekend to Midhurst. The news was with us in no time and after that he had little control.

The camp then developed new problems. One morning as I went out at half past seven an Australian girl sprang out from the bushes outside our house.

"I must leave at once," she said.

"Good heavens," I replied, startled. "Good heavens, why?"

"I can't tell you, but my friend and I have quarrelled". She had come with two other girls.

Two mornings later as I came out of the front door another Australian girl was waiting there. She too pounced on me and insisted on leaving at once. As she had a car, which is always valuable in a camp, I did my best to get her to stay.

"What is wrong?" I said. "Two of you leaving like this. That will leave only one girl in the caravan".

"Then Jacques and she," she said bitterly, "can do just as they like every night".

Jacques was a good looking French boy of twenty-three. He had slept with the first girl on the Monday night and with the second girl on the Tuesday, after which the first girl sprang out of the bushes at me. On the fourth night he had slept with the third girl after which the second one had pounced on me.

"What disgraceful behaviour," said Paula. "You must sack him at once; we can't have things like that happening in the camp".

"I'm not going to sack him," I said. "He is an excellent worker and a very nice fellow; we are short of people. Anyhow, it wasn't his fault".

Jacques was sharing a caravan with a couple of English boys and to our astonishment an invitation came up for us to dine with them that night. Intrigued I accepted and Paula reluctantly agreed to come with me.

The caravan looked lovely. The table was set with cutlery, flowers and glasses. There were candles in the necks of wine bottles. Jacques gave us French onion soup, trout and ended the meal with a fluffy sweet omelette. The supply of wine was liberal and good. Jacques paid special

attention to Paula all the evening.

As we walked back up to the house Paula said,

"You know I don't think Jacques was to blame. It was the fault of those stupid girls".

Jacques stayed and was very popular. When he left and I drove him to the station all the girls turned out to wave him goodbye and what was astonishing was that the men liked him too. He

should have gone on the films. Perhaps
he did.

★ ★ ★

I always try and book in at least one
African or Indian though I did not accept
fifteen Mau-Mau when they applied en
bloc during the terrible Kenya troubles.
Nowadays the race relations board would
be after me for that.

One year I booked in a Pakistani. As
I was driving up the lane I passed a tall
figure carrying a rucksack. He was clearly
my Pakistani and I stopped and picked
him up.

"You're not a Pakistani," I said in
Urdu, "you are a Pathan".

He had the bearing of the North
Indian fighting man and he came from
one of that small ruling elite of some
fifty families who seem to take it in
turns to govern Pakistan. The former
East Pakistanis, now Bangladeshies, are
an entirely different breed — small and
dark skinned.

My Pathan was amusing and well
mannered but a hopeless worker. When

261

I tackled him he said.

"You put me on piece work, Sahib, and it will not matter, I enjoy it here and wish to stay".

Then he went on, "I've watched many films of the old British Raj and in them the English officers speak a special sort of Urdu. You Sahib speak in exactly that manner. I never thought to hear it in real life".

When he was finally due to leave, having earned very little pay, we had him in to dinner.

"I had not realised Sahib," he said, "that you expected so much work. If I had been warned I would have brought two or three girls with me and by their working long hours while I supervised I would have received much pay".

On Saturday mornings, rather like a District Commissioner in India, I would set up a table in the middle of the camp. On it would be bags of coins and bundles of notes. Pay for the camp was complicated because people might have done apple picking, overtime, tractor driving and pack house work. Ninety per cent of the details put in by each camper would be accurate and honest. Some campers however were so illiterate that their time sheets needed detailed discussion; and there would usually be one who was deliberately overclaiming.

Paula would inspect the caravans, some ten of which in those days we hired in addition to the five we owned. We had to return them in spotless condition or we ourselves would have to pay a penalty. Paula as a doctor was used to the hygienic condition of hospital wards. On the first inspection only two or three caravans would be passed by her for payment of wages. The camp site also had to be cleaned up and this included tins which people had thrown out of their back windows and the broken glass in the fire where someone had thrown a bottle. Cooking stoves were the main problem. It must have been the first time that some of the campers had met a demand for real cleanliness.

The problem was to enforce discipline without setting the camp against us. We were entirely dependent on their willingness to work and we had to keep them on our side. It was a delicate balance and one could only afford to be really tough each week with one or two of the worst offenders. Fortunately we always had some people who kept their caravans and their time sheets immaculate; these were soon paid off and this had an effect on the others. It was very time consuming and exhausting, and at the end of the long week we would retire exhausted to bed for the afternoon.

Twenty years later cleanliness in the caravans continues to be a sore point. In my letter of engagement I state that I will not pay on Saturday mornings until the caravans are clean. People's ideas of cleanliness vary considerably. I always expect Scottish girls to be clean, but I had one recently who, although pretty and clean herself, hadn't the beginnings of an idea about cleanliness. On the stove grease built up steadily. Each week I threatened to deduct money from her but relented. She tried a little harder but her boyfriend, also clean in himself, had as dirty caravan habits as she had. In the end I deducted ten pounds and it took one of our best members of staff three hours to clean the stove, let alone the caravan.

We only accept telephone messages for campers in emergencies. Late at night we may get a call.

"May I speak to Richard Brompton, please?"

"No, he's a quarter of a mile away in a caravan. Is it urgent?"

"Yes, it is very urgent".

"How urgent, is someone seriously ill or dead?"

Urgency so often means making a date for next week but the question of a death makes them think and then they usually give the reason for the call, which of course may be urgent.

In the early sixties we had a young man who came back to us three times. He was well educated and had the fashionable idealistic views of the time which, unlike most people, he unwisely put into practice. His mother and father were on our wavelength but their son considered them hopeless. The telephone would go.

"This is Julian's mother, I feel foolish to ask, but have you any news of him?"

one Scottish girl although clean and
pretty herself, hadn't the beginnings
of an idea of cleanliness.

"Yes, Julian is in prison in Greece".

"Oh dear, what for?"

"For demonstrating against the Colonels, but I hear he is due out soon and is coming to us in four weeks time".

A year would pass and much the same conversation would take place.

"Yes, Julian I understand is in prison in Paris".

"Oh dear, what for this time?"

"A student demonstration against the police, but he is due out and is coming here."

We quite missed him when he ceased going to prison and coming on here. I expect he is now a model of domesticity.

★ ★ ★

1966

One of our bookings half way through a camp was from Lord Jeremy Brown, it was a courtesy title and a genuine one. He was a younger son.

He arrived one hot Sunday afternoon when the packing shed was working. He uncoiled six foot four inches of good looking manhood from a low green open MGA. The girls, who were mostly from the Dominions, watched fascinated — a real young Lord. The camp quickly encapsulated him and within a few days the girls were teasing him a great deal. He took it in good part, and certainly did not use his title as girl bait.

He turned out to be rather dumb but very brave. Each night when the pubs closed the leather jacketed motorcyclists would try to get into the farm. I had had a solid gate erected at the bottom of the drive but the problem was to get our van and cars in without them following. Unasked Jeremy took on the job. Leaping out of his MG he would face the following motorcycles, wave our cars through and then swing shut and padlock the heavy gate. His great height and confident attitude prevented any fighting.

In the early days pickers' pay was too low for income tax and one was charged 6 pence in the pound to cover their

National Insurance. As pay has gone up and tax allowances have become relatively smaller most pickers are due to pay tax and insurance and it is the growers' duty to collect it. From our campers tales it is clear that in the hotel trade many workers are paid cash in the hand without the deductions due.

My training as a Chartered Accountant and a healthy streak of fear in me has, however, meant that both I and my staff pay in full the taxes due. The Inland Revenue, the National Insurance and the VAT people pounce every few years on farmers and their methods are quite remarkably astute.

Last year the tax people had wind of a Suffolk farm which made no deductions. Thirty officers crept up and surrounded the field of pickers who, on seeing the trap, ran for it in all directions. The strawberries were never picked.

A few years ago Holland brought in on pickers the same tax regulations as those under which we suffer. As a result the Dutch blackcurrant crop dropped by 80% in two years and large acreages were pulled out.

When negotiating in a heated office on this tax with Whitehall officials on behalf of the fruit industry all of us four farmers took off our coats while the pale officials kept theirs on. We found them a difficult bunch, out of touch with reality.

★ ★ ★

1968

When I bought Toat Lodge the Lordship of the Manor was included in the title deeds. With the deeds came a history of a long feud which had been going on for over a hundred years with a local family who also claimed the Lordship. The two sides must have spent many hundreds of pounds in solicitor's fees. We fired off one or two desultory shots at the other side which they countered. Then my excellent solicitor, Eric Thompson, suggested a change of plan, which was to end in tragedy.

"Let us," he said, "present them with a fait accompli and force them to attack our position. I will write formally to their solicitors saying that on December 10th at 12.00 o'clock you intend as Lord of the Manor to exercise your rights of timber on Thorn Common. Meanwhile you mark one of the large oak trees with white paint and announce that you plan to fell it at that time. It'll be up to them to try and stop you".

I agreed and Eric duly wrote receiving in reply a letter denying my rights of timber. Two or three letters passed but nothing forceful came from the other side. The other claimant was over eighty and I heard from my staff that he was becoming very agitated over the developing situation. I wondered whether we should pull back. I telephoned Eric.

"You must push on David," he said. "The situation has become quite ridiculous and needs to be settled one way or the other".

Meanwhile as Lord of the Manor I was negotiating with a local pub for a rent for parking cars on the common land. To my surprise they offered me six bottles of whisky a year, but I didn't accept as I felt we should wait for the outcome of the tree felling.

The great oak was duly felled at 12.00

o'clock. It went down with a heart rending crash (I have replaced it). The timber fellers started cleaning the trunk, stacking the cords of wood and burning up the frith. (Small branches which in the old days were used in ovens for baking bread.) At half past twelve the news was brought to me that the other claimant had died of a heart attack. What can one do in such a position? One cannot write and apologise. I did nothing and the two families let the situation lie for several years. I did however gather from the wife of one of my staff who worked for the other family that they bore me no grudge.

After some years the son of the other claimant telephoned me.

"I think we should settle this business of the Lord of the Manor. Going through my father's affairs I see that he paid out big solicitor's fees down the years, and I expect your side have done the same."

After some consultation we agreed to give our solicitors instructions to meet and to come to a decision within one day. We were to put all our cards on the table and to accept the decision, whatever it might be.

I telephoned Eric to tell him what had been arranged.

"That's marvellous," he said, "we cannot fail to win, I have been through all the papers and they are sound as a bell." The solicitors duly met. Late that evening Eric rang me up.

"The most extraordinary thing," he said, "you both have exactly equal rights. The Lordship of the Manor was left to twin sisters. Each sister's share has come down along the line to the two of you. You are joint Lords of the Manor."

The two of us agreed to divide the Manor along the line of Pickhurst Lane. I took all the verges and common land of Toat to the north and he took all the verges of D'Albiac to the south, together with the common land in front of the local pub, the one which had offered me the whisky.

Since that date we have never disputed or disturbed each other's rights. Manor lordships are recognised by members of the House of Lords and the College of Arms.

The main right that I acquired was the "timber" and "sporting" of Thorn common. This is the best bit of shooting in the valley. There are only three commoners and they have rights only of hook and crook, which means that they can pick up fallen timber and pull down dead branches, but they cannot cut branches off for firewood. The road across the common is only open to commoners and by the use of my Manor rights I have been able to stop two efforts at development. The rights of "primae noctis" or first night with girl commoners are sadly no longer exercisable.

* * *

When I started farming there were hardly any bullfinches in Sussex but Kent was full of them, and they were reported to be moving west in great strength at about thirty miles a year. None of us would grudge a bullfinch a little food but when they peck fruit buds they only take a tiny bit of the centre and spit out the rest. They work at lightning speed clearing each branch completely

There are only three commoners

before they move to the next. A flock of bullfinches can devastate an acre a day and as they take every bud, those trees will not have any fruit that year. With plums the buds are often killed and the tree can never recover. The birds are justifiably feared.

From our area we watched with interest as a grower in East Sussex started the defence. There is a chardoneret bullfinch trap which if baited with bloody veined dock, or if placed beside a decoy bird rarely catches anything else. All my friend's staff were given these traps and a tame bird; and were paid for each bullfinch caught. The bodies were sent off to Oxford University which was doing a study on this pest.

If the position had not been so desperate no grower would have resorted to these methods. They had first tried protective black cotton strung across the trees. It is put on five lines at a time with a special tool, and for a few days baffles the bullfinches. They soon learn however and fly over the treated trees into the centre of the orchards.

During the course of this campaign the grower had a great deal of trouble with trespassing locals and in the end the RSPCA impounded all his decoy birds, which by then were family pets. A prosecution was brought but the case was fought by the National Farmers Union and the grower won. The RSPCA were ordered to return the bullfinches which they did; all of them were dead of starvation.

As suddenly and mysteriously as they had come the bullfinches retreated back to Kent. Shortly afterwards Dr Newton of Oxford University published a treatise on bullfinch habits based on the bodies sent to him. The birds do not take fruit buds until they have finished all the nettle, blackberry and ash seeds. Some years there is sufficient ash seed to feed them all winter and then fruit trees everywhere are safe.

Why did the bullfinches retreat to Kent? Why did all the bluetits in England one year learn to pick holes in milk bottle tops? Why did Bramley apples, normally scab resistant, in one year everywhere become subject to scab? Nature is difficult to understand.

★ ★ ★

In the 1950's and 1960's there were no herbicides available. We kept our orchard cut with a five tier gang mower. These are complicated and expensive machines but when in good order run like a dream. The men drove at something like twelve miles an hour only slowing down to swing round the corners. The plume of grass sprayed out across the orchard floor and was taken in by the worms. We had to trim round each tree by hand and that was a heartbreaking and endless job. The swap hook used is the same as the sickle of Russia. It is one of the oldest tools in history, going back in its present shape for at least six thousand years. It was the reaping tool of the ancient Egyptians and of China. In England it is used with a "hooky" stick cut from the hedgerow and the secret of its use is to keep it sharp.

To reduce the endless labour of trimming around the trees the first invention was a swing wing to the mower. A projecting lever touched the trunk of the tree and swung the wing back and around it. The arrival of herbicides was a godsend but I am still not convinced that they are harmless. We use as little as possible and I have seen with relief that most of them do not harm worms. Any that do we have never used again, Can one trust scientists?

9

Badgers, Wild Life and Drainage

IT was not until I had been in the country for ten years that I began to understand that the farm that I owned on paper was shared with other owners. Badgers, deer, foxes, hawks, owls, robins, partridge and numerous other animals and birds are territorial. A family of black hunting cats owned twenty acres to the east of the farm while a different family owned a similar area to the west. The middle of the farm has never been claimed. Hunting cats are one of our fiercest predators, and although they look the same as domestic ones, are very different.

One year our campers had taken up a kitten and named it unimaginatively "Cat". During December while we were away we had two girls staying in the house; they brought Cat in. When we got back he was firmly established.

"You knew," I said, "we didn't want that cat in the house, he isn't a domestic cat."

"Oh Mr. Atkins," replied the prettiest one. "We thought you wouldn't mind. Cat was so cold outside and so miserable, and we do love having him with us."

Cat was so cold outside and so miserable

"You can take him into your caravan and let's hope he stops there."

But he didn't; he could always find a way into our house and our cat-hating dog was soon rocked back on his heels by a slash across the nose. Cat was here to stay.

Our garden has always been a haven for birds but now day after day Cat would bring in dead chaffinches, great tits, coal tits and robins. He rarely caught sparrows, those ragamuffins of the bird world.

Paula found it intolerable and we gave him away to a farmer some ten miles distant. He had five or six hunting cats which kept his barns free of rats and mice. Within ten days Cat was back asleep in the airing cupboard on my recently ironed dress shirt.

Next time we gave him away to a farmer some twenty-five miles away. This time it took Cat four weeks to get back. He returned not because he regarded our house as his home, but to re-establish the ownership of his territory. He was now a real problem but as we knew he could live anywhere in the wild, we didn't have the heart to put him down. In the end I drove him fifty miles away and turned him out in a wood. He stumped off angrily flicking his tail at me as he went.

Weasels and stoats have their own areas as do families of rabbits. When one watches the extreme territorial possessiveness of so many birds and animals one realises that human ownership of land is only temporary and that to change the environment is an interference with the rights of wildlife and plants.

Both our farms have badger setts on or near them. Badger territories are very large, extending I would guess to about two hundred acres for each sett. They are strong animals, not very agile but very determined. Where the fox and deer will leap over a rabbit fence the badger will go straight through it, tearing the wire apart or digging it up. All rabbit fencing is dug into the ground six inches before it turns at right angles outwards for another six inches. This baffles rabbits but not badgers. The only answer is to give them their own private doorway like a big catflap. We have a number of these on the farm. They are eighteen inches square and swing both ways. The badgers quickly learn to use them but rabbits, intelligent as they are, regard them with suspicion and will never push through them. Rabbits have however learnt to jump and fences now have to be higher than they used to be.

Badgers dig shallow lavatory pits but never fill them in. Rabbits prefer, when dunging, to sit on the top of a rise in

Rabbits regard them with suspicion

the ground where they can see around them. They use the same place again and again. Foxes are deliberately impertinent and, to annoy the dogs, will dung close to our house. Our dogs avoid dunging in the garden and it makes them very cross to find foxes' droppings there. Deer seem to do it anywhere.

* * *

In the 1950's and 1960's the field drainage grant was fifty per cent. We then recovered a third of the balance in tax refunds. This meant that the final cost was £33.00 out of each £100. All over England large acreages were improved by new drains and at Tullens over ten years we did all the fields. We used the 3″ tile drains at a depth of 2′ 9″. These were filled up to 12″ below ground level with gravel. One then drew mole drains at 2′ depth through the gravel at right angles. With the mole drains 6′ apart the clay soil could shed surplus water easily. The three Streeter brothers who put in all our drains used the special tools for the job. There are numerous types of spade and fork used for different purposes in farming and the drainage spade is thin and tapering. Drains must have an exact fall and a scoop is used to take out the last inch or so, then the drain is tested with a bucket of water for its flow and finally the 1′ long pipes are laid with a special tool. How I miss those three brothers who would ditch my farm far more speedily than a tractor and digger. Unless the soil is basically sound no amount of drainage will really improve the heavy yellow and blue clays of the Weald. Fortunately our soil is better structured than most; it has higher aeration and easier movement of water but it still remains difficult to farm. It is no use ploughing clay fields in the spring; it must be done in the autumn and then the winter frost will break up the soil and do the work for you.

When draining we came across the old 2″ drains which were put in during the three agricultural depressions of the nineteenth century. There was then no unemployment pay and the great landowners came to the rescue by building park walls and draining all their fields. There must have been a Government grant of some sort for in the farm next to mine the 2″ drains are sham. The outfalls are there but after about 20 ft of drain there is nothing. The contractors or the landowner had drawn the grant but not put in the drains.

General Renton, when he was digging out the ditches on his very heavy clay soil struck a drain at the depth of 5 ft. He searched further and found that the whole of his farm was drained at this level; he was able to reconstitute the system which probably dated to the early 1800's. Really old drain systems do not have round drain pipes but half round ones laid on flat stones. All old systems are one chain or two chains apart (a chain is twenty two feet), so if you find one chain you can probably find the others.

In any agricultural depression the first economy is on the maintenance of ditches. These then clog up above the outfalls, and the drain fills with standing water out of which the clay particles precipitate; within ten years the drain is blocked solid. To get them to run again is not as difficult as one would expect. If the outfall is kept clear the water seeping in between the one foot long pipes will gradually clear the drain from the outfall backwards. It can be assisted by rodding and now I believe by crawling water jets.

Now that in 1991 we are again in a severe agricultural depression all the drainage work that took place in the 1950's and 60's is likely to be let go. When the tide turns again and food is wanted, the next generation of farmers may be able to find the drains again as, since the war, all drainage schemes have been mapped and filed with the Ministry of Agriculture. Since the grant has been stopped little drainage work has been done anywhere in England.

It can be assisted by rodding

The drainage grant was the only subsidy we have ever got. Since 1950 fruit growers have relied on open market prices, and without any help from our Government, have often had to combat subsidised apples exported from all over Europe and America.

* * *

When I had come back from Rhodesia where I had played polo, I found myself welcome at such clubs as Ham, Jericho Priory, Henley and others. There were few people in England in 1953 who knew the game and with my poor handicap of -2, I was asked to play as No 1 in many public matches. I was in demand because at a moment's notice I was prepared to ride any strange horse for any club. I was never charged for any of my mounts. I had even raised my own team "Rossetti House" for the low handicap tournament at Rhinefield.

I had only two polo sticks and with so many different horses to ride I used to borrow suitable sticks from other players, chiefly Jimmy Edwards. This was alright until his girl friend, bored with watching his West End play night after night, started dropping in at my tiny flat near Harrods and we cooked supper together.

"Can I borrow a long stick, Jimmy, one of my ponies is over 16 hands?"

"No you bloody can't," replied Jimmy and I had to play the pony with a short stick.

In spite of his reputation, I believe that behind that great moustache lurked a romantic.

In the early 60s a few locals started a new polo club. It had only one rule, no horse could be bought for over £300. I got a former polo pony from Cowdray but, lacking a groom, never got her fit. She was always too fat, and anyhow I have never understood horses but when overseas relied on my syces.

We played on a big field lent by the Dutton-Forshaws. It went quite well for a while and we fended off efforts by the press to herald it as a fashionable new club.

The odd thing about the club was that so many of the members' houses were burgled. Then one day one of the playing wives was hurt and was carried up to the Dutton-Forshaws main bedroom. Her husband naturally went up to see her. Three days later when the Dutton-Forshaws were watching television they heard a noise upstairs. They rushed up and saw a man leaping out of the window. As he ran across the garden in the gloaming, he looked vaguely familiar. It was the member whose wife had been hurt. The police pounced and found his house was full of stolen silver, jewels and china, much of it from the other members' houses. He went to jail, but it was not exactly a boost for the club.

Finally my horse bucked me off. I flew in an arc and fell on my head. Fortunately I rolled but with only a few inches different in the angle of fall my neck would have been broken. I was frightened and Paula was upset. I realised I was getting older and I gave up polo.

★ ★ ★

Now that the fashion for planting is in densities of 1600 trees or more to the acre, the cost of the stake has become very relevant. The hurricane of 1987 which struck when the leaves were still on, brought great pressure on the trees and many people with thin stakes lost whole orchards. We escaped with damage, but without a disaster.

Almost all stakes used to be cut from chestnut coppice. These are harvested in rotation every fourteen years and, unlike hazel coppice, are still in demand. Early on an excellent picker put me in touch with her husband who worked the Stopham Estate woods. He was a true countryman and with him there was never any doubt about quality or sizes. I am glad to say that those woods, with their drifts of wild daffodils, are still being coppiced regularly for fencing stakes as they have been for hundreds of years.

Later, as we planted more trees to the acre, we used the cheaper tanalised softwoods. Specifications in England are on the diameter at the top of the stake but on the continent they are on the diameter at the bottom of the stake — a cause of great misunderstanding. 2″ diameter at the top is too thin and over 3″ a stake is too stout to be driven

a cause of great misunderstanding

in easily. I order 2½″ minimum, 3″ maximum, but sometimes some of the stakes are below specification. As long as one hasn't paid, one has the whiphand.

A load delivered from the Queen's estate at Windsor looked all right and I paid. A year later they started to break, they had been treated wrongly and were brittle. Her Estate Manager replaced the stakes with an apology. The letters from Windsor had the Queen's special mark; she does not use stamps. At about this time I was also, to my surprise, telephoned by a member of the

Queen's Household.

"Should we pull out the orchards at Sandringham?" he asked.

"I don't know the orchards but I have frequently seen her apples in the market. They will never be a success, they are too small and lack colour."

The orchards were changed to 'pick your own' and to farmgate sales. They survive only on the Queen's name.

★ ★ ★

1969

In my opening talk to campers I mention that if there is any trouble locally the police will come first to us. In particular I ask them not to take signs from outside shops or paraffin lamps from roadworks.

There is always someone who does not listen. One year up came the police.

"You know there's a foot and mouth standstill down Findon way?"

"Yes," I said, "but I've got no cattle."

"A lot of signs have gone, have you seen them?"

"No, but you are welcome to search

the camp. They won't be here, I have spoken about signs", but there they were, piled neatly behind the caravan of the two who had taken them. The campers were prosecuted, fined and given a conditional discharge. It was a wicked thing to have done.

On another occasion the police turned up in force, three car loads of them. "Oh dear," I said, "what have the campers done now?"

"We think there is an escaped prisoner in your camp".

"I am sure there isn't but please feel free to search".

In ten minutes they were back with a bedraggled looking man. He had been hiding in one of the caravans for four days. The sense of camaraderie among campers to all those who are down on their luck is really quite extraordinary and I suppose in some ways admirable.

Our farm van has always been only too well known to the police. No one is allowed to use it without my permission, and this is given for shopping and going out to pubs in the evening. If they are going far I need to know to where and for what reason. We check the mileage as we have had people taking the van to London.

The telephone went, "This is the Brighton police speaking, I gather your van is white with a blue flash on it."

"That's right," I replied, "but it's in Horsham at the moment".

"No, it's not, it's in Brighton on a double yellow line."

"Don't say you'll charge me with a traffic offence?" I asked.

"No," replied the police, "to avoid that we will charge the driver with stealing the van" and so they did to the amazed indignation of the camper. I repeat this story regularly to campers, and I think it has some effect.

★ ★ ★

Since they had found the escaped prisoner in our caravans, the police paid us regular and welcome visits. In the course of one of these they noticed that several of the old cars in camp were using Guinness labels instead of licences. These used to be much the same colour and shape.

I had warned the campers that the local police were very hot on licences and most of the cars stayed in camp. When the last day came, however, the police must have lain in wait. Six cars with false licences set out from our farm, three were stopped within two miles, two further on at Billingshurst, and only one reached London. Nowadays unlicensed cars, in fact any cars at all, in the camp are rare. Occasionally we have camper vans; there is a street market in London used chiefly by New Zealanders who meet weekly and buy and sell vans.

We bought one of the camper's cars for ten pounds, and our children drove it all over the farm. An off duty policeman picking strawberries was astonished to see an apparently driverless vehicle coming up our farm road. It was John, aged nine and only just able to see out through the steering wheel. I was admonished under some regulation and after that our boys could only drive where the public had no access. I have found the local police helpful.

Many New Zealanders have farm repair and building experience and one of our best couples stayed for several months. At the end he and his girlfriend each bought a Mercedes with the money they had saved and borrowed. On exporting it to New Zealand they not merely saved the VAT, but were able to sell the car for a very high profit.

★ ★ ★

In 1968 the Government asked for evidence to be given to a Select Committee on Agriculture. I submitted a short memorandum. To my surprise I got a telephone call asking me to attend. When I arrived in the House of Commons the assembled journalists asked me who I was. "I am an apple grower" I replied.

"Yes," they said, "but who do you represent?"

"I represent myself".

A journalist explained to me.

"We have had evidence from the Ministry of Agriculture, the Board of Trade, London University, The Produce Packers Association, the National Farmers Union, and now you turn up and say you just represent yourself".

"That's correct," I replied, "that's what I am, an independent grower with no ties".

John Wells was in the chair and the others were John Farr, John Dunwoody and Derek Page. Everyone else giving evidence had come backed by officials. Before answering any questions they thought long and hard. I had no idea that every word I said, and I mean every incautious word, would be taken down, printed and published. An early question was:

"What is your attitude to the statutory grading provisions?"

"One of the most useless regulations ever put on the Statute Book. There is no advantage to anyone. It employs one hundred and seventy civil servants who would be better working elsewhere. If they all left tomorrow they would not be missed in the slightest".

"What would you do with the one hundred and seventy staff?"

"I hope I would not see them re-employed within the Ministry. I hope they would go back on to the labour market where they are so badly needed".

The committee cross-examined me for the whole morning particularly on my statement that on September 5th 1958 and May 31st 1964, hail had cost me over £20,000, and that on May 5th 1961 and May 2nd 1967, frost had lost me over £30,000. Each occasion necessitated the cancelling at once of large items of capital expenditure. When the proceedings were published it brought some repercussions. Some six months later I was present when John Wells was being questioned by the press on his final report.

"The cross-examination of Mr Atkins reads very strangely," said a questioner. "Was it of any use?"

"Yes it was," replied John Wells, "we found his off the cuff remarks gave us an insight into an apple grower's problems which a more formal approach would not have revealed".

Afterwards the Treasury got in touch with me and, for farmers, brought in the averaging of two years profits which both the NFU and I had suggested; this has been most helpful.

★ ★ ★

When we reached the peak of our acreage we were getting a thousand tons of Cox a year. A thousand tons is the load that is carried in a long goods train. To pick them we had to expand from our basic staff of six to over one hundred and still keep control. During one particular crop I woke in the early morning.

"Are you awake?" I whispered to Paula.

"Yes," she said, "wide awake".

"We are not going to get the crop in with the pickers we've got, are we?"

"No, we're certainly not".

"We've got to do something".

"Perhaps we should advertise widely," she said.

"All right let's do it thoroughly. Could you put it tomorrow in every local paper in Brighton to Crawley, Midhurst, Chichester and all the coast towns. We'll take on everybody who answers".

Then followed the most extraordinary two weeks. The telephone rang so frequently that we hardly had time to eat or snatch a cup of coffee. We took on twenty people a day and, what was far more exhausting, I was sacking somebody every hour of daylight. A lot of riff raff had turned up. One complaint from a supervisor, the slightest argument, one badly bruised box of apples and they were out. We had no time to give anyone a second chance. In the end we had two hundred and twenty four people on the payroll.

The staff, who were picking up the boxes on to trailers, kept account in rent books. From these they were consolidated daily into the main records. Three drivers might each pick up twice a day from each picker, so it was quite a job. All the pickers had work sheets which showed their name, their picking number and the boxes they claimed to have picked each day.

On the final day a storm threatened and the skies darkened. As each orchard was finished the supervisors brought in their pickers to the last orchard, Stable Field. In the end we had one hundred and fifty people all picking in three acres. Half an hour before we would have finished the skies opened, the lightning flashed and down came the torrential rain. All our tractor drivers' books were soaked and smudged. We did not know who had picked what and had no way of checking it.

I knew that most people were honest in their claims for boxes picked. Many of the pickers had nobly stayed out in the rain to finish the orchard and now they came in soaking wet. Piles of money stood on the table in front of me. When paying out big amounts I used to keep a shotgun, unloaded, behind me, with ammunition in my pocket.

I had the supervisors with their useless books beside me. I asked each picker:

"How many boxes today?" Most who were known as reliable I paid out at once. For the few others I turned to the supervisors.

"Do you agree that?"

They had been told to disagree with the figures and I knocked each claim down by a few boxes. If however the

we gave them all a free box of apples

picker thought it unfair, I paid out. I don't think they cheated me by much if at all.

Although they were all soaking wet the crowd were good tempered because they knew that, against all the odds, they had succeeded in getting in the crop. They had a sense of achievement and I showed my gratitude. We gave them all a free box of apples.

Picking appeals to the squirrelling instinct of human beings and there are very few people who do not enjoy harvesting. It is an ancient race memory and, even if they don't recognise it at first, everybody has it. They find themselves caught up by the feeling they are doing something natural which will help feed their group through the winter to come.

For the English apple grower the narrow dates within which the crop has to be 'got' presents a major problem. Harvest is easy for the South Africans, the New Zealanders and the Americans who all have several main varieties which crop over a long period. The Cox, which is so temperamental, is our main apple. It crops in England at a maximum of ten tons an acre while all other commercial varieties throughout the world crop regularly at between twenty and thirty tons per acre.

My son, who spent six months' working on a fruit farm in South Africa, remarked that because of their warm summer and extended season they had no problems with getting the trees to crop and so their pruning was very simple. Their growing does not have to be so precise but the quality of their packing and marketing is very good. With their high production they sell on the English market, receive the proceeds in pounds, and pay their expenses in cheap rand. They thus make very heavy profits per acre, indeed fantastic profits of some ten times as much as the best growers in England can achieve.

★ ★ ★

1970

In one camp two good looking young men arrived in a sports car. They worked alright, but were out every night at pubs and each Friday evening went off to London. I had another visit from the police.

"There's a great deal of stealing of pictures from the pubs. I think it's probably something to do with your campers."

I spoke to the camp and next day a girl came up secretly to the house to speak to me. She had seen the men take pictures and a dagger from a pub wall. I informed the police, but the men had already vanished without collecting their pay. They left one thing behind, a threatening note to the girl.

"We'll come back and get you, you little bitch," it read. Poor girl she couldn't sleep and soon left. How they knew it was her I have no idea.

Before we had showers down at the camp we used to let campers come in on a half hour roster system two at a time to use our bathrooms. With the big boiler roaring as hard as it could go they were able to get reasonably hot baths. The system had one advantage; if anyone wanted to speak to us privately they could, when they came up for a bath, knock at our door.

In every camp there are some people who are not properly house trained and the baths would sometimes not be washed out and hair left in the plug holes. The final crunch came when Paula found someone had used her toothbrush. Next year we built two shower rooms.

That year I took on a Welsh girl from a mining family. It was a heavy crop and half way through we decided to increase the camp numbers. We hired another eight caravans, advertised, and took on twenty four extra people. In a four berth caravan three strangers are the maximum who can live in amity.

Our camp contact was a liaison camper, Ken, a rather useless Englishman who lived practically entirely off our failed sweetcorn crop. He had been with us before which was the reason for his appointment.

On the arrival of the new campers there was some trouble in settling in and Ken asked if he could come up and see me with Ellie, the girl from the Welsh coal fields. They came up and we gave them both a drink.

I was so exhausted by the crop that, as I sipped my large whisky, I did not really take in what Ellie was saying.

"I speak," she said aggressively, "for the senior campers. When the crop is over we must have dismissals on a last in first out basis."

"Of course, of course," I muttered, thinking of tomorrow's threatened rain.

"There's to be no overtime offered to new campers until all the senior campers have been offered it and refused."

"Seems reasonable," I said, leaning back and wondering when tonight's lorry would arrive.

"Finally," said Ellie, "No new camper is to have a bath in your house. We have booked all the places."

"The boiler won't cope with any more, so that's all right," I replied.

Ellie and Ken were out of the house before Paula exploded.

"Do you realise you have lost control of the camp? Sacking, overtime and baths are vital."

"Oh, did I agree to all that?" I said,

helping myself to a second whisky.

"You certainly did. Go down now and speak to the camp." I'd never seen her so angry.

I told the next person on the bath list to go back and to get everyone assembled in ten minutes.

I went down, my talk was short.

"There's been an effort on the part of a few campers to divide you into two groups, new arrivals and old. Everyone here will be judged only on their work. I want it clearly understood that I run the camp, I decide who stays and who goes, I decide who has overtime, and I decide who has baths. Anyone not agreeing to these terms may leave tomorrow morning,

Anyone wish to leave?"

Ellie withdrew into the background, but to my amazement applied the following year to come again. I refused her.

10

Foreign Orchards and Boxes

AT the time when the planting up of Golden Delicious was going ahead fast twenty of us went on a fruit tour to France. I have always loved France; its stability lies in its high proportion of good soil jealously held by families who are capable of almost complete self sufficiency. We quickly realised how easy it was for them to grow apples. They had high yielding varieties and with a warm climate had no problem either with size or with pollination.

We noticed one great difference between English and French farms. When one goes on an orchard walk on an English farm the talk is given and questions answered either by the owner or by his manager. If there is a Ministry of Agriculture official present, he is there as a guest. When one goes to a French farm the Ministry official gives the lecture, answers the questions and is the man in authority. Only when the questions become too technical does he turn and call on first the Cooperative director and then as a last resort the owner who emerges from the background. One's impression of the owners was of small and shabbily dressed men who were in awe of the Ministry and of the Cooperative executives.

This situation seems to run all through France. Their civil servants run the countryside and their objective is to do the best for France. In England the Ministry of Agriculture fulfils the role of helpful advisor on whom one may or may not call. At top levels the Ministry tends not to fight for British interests but to treat every problem from an international viewpoint. This may be a relic of the British Empire and it certainly acts against the interests of the English farmer who rarely has anyone to fight his corner against the Dutch, French, German and Italian farmers. We feel our Government can be relied upon not to help us.

An Englishman who four years ago

bought a vineyard near the Pyrenees, was advised by the maire to take out all his vines. He did so and on signing the village document was handsomely paid.

The next year he was asked to sign again and was paid again. The third year he signed again and was paid again.

On protesting to the maire he was told that he must sign or none of the villagers would be paid.

"The Italians," said the maire, "are

small shabbily dressed men in awe of the Ministry and Co operative executives

normally paid five times for each olive tree they take out and we expect to get the same or more."

The funds were paid by the EEC and much of that would end up on English backs.

The French on the tour were most hospitable and they ended up by giving us an excellent lunch in the Camargue. We were served delicious octopus which many growers did not have the courtesy to taste. After lunch immature bulls were brought out and several of our party tried their hands at bull fighting. Our leader had a stout German wife. She was chatting with her back to the ring when a young bull charged straight at me. I sidestepped smartly and he took her fair and square on her bottom. Fortunately she was not hurt but when again on her feet she looked sourly at me.

"David, a gentleman would have stood his ground". To do me justice I did not know she was directly behind me, and anyhow I did not see how I could stop a charging bull.

Her husband, a man of great charm, was for many years the leader of our apple industry. He had an eight hundred acre farm and I asked him if I could take a party to see it. He was strangely reluctant and as soon as we stepped on to the farm I could see why. It was a complete mess. Of the thirty staff half of them were employed in repairing the numerous cottages and barns. Many of the mowers and sprayers were out of order. The owner himself, who was Lord Lieutenant of his County, had handed over the management to his son with whom I travelled the farm.

"I am a one ulcer man with a four ulcer job," he said. "We have vast assets and no income".

"What is your rate of production?" I asked.

"Under a hundred boxes per acre," he said. "I hope it won't go higher as if it does we won't be able to pick or store the crop".

We saw over their cold stores. The walls had been made with concrete poured around ping pong balls. It worked well and was very cheap.

The farm was a lesson not to be tempted to overplant. A couple of years later when the son resigned in despair, the family sold off three quarters of the farm and some fifteen cottages. This left them plenty of capital and far fewer problems but they vanished out of fruit growing.

★ ★ ★

1975

Nothing is more disastrous than to have apples unpicked and to run out of containers. With an average crop of sixty thousand boxes we had to find the money to buy them in advance. A lorry load holds one thousand two hundred boxes, today worth 80p each. We would have fifty piles ranged along the quarter mile drive to the house. For fire safety each pile had to be separate. Boxes nest in threes but take up an awful lot of room. When one saw the wall of boxes it seemed impossible that we should ever fill them. Nowadays we pick into wooden bins each holding 600 lbs of fruit.

Boxes became an obsession with me. People sat on them and broke them, they stood on them and broke them, they drove tractors over them, they put them down in the mud, they threw them casually off trailers, and the greatest crime of all — they burnt them in the caravan stoves or on the bonfires. My arrival lecture to the camp mentioned this crime as a sacking offence.

One night I was awakened by the light of a bonfire some two hundred yards away. The light did not look like branches burning, it was too white. Putting on my dressing gown and wellington boots I stumped down to the camp at two o'clock in the morning. There were three of them, drunk, piling boxes onto the fire. They were startled at my fury. If they had not been bigger than me I would have hit them.

"You will leave at nine a.m. tomorrow," I said and stumped back to bed, but not to sleep. It is this sort of thing that is so draining during a crop.

The box manufacturers, if they got the main order in March, would give an option to increase the order at the end of June. This is the first moment one can estimate the crop. If one does not get the crop estimate right one might, disaster, be left in early October with every apple container in England full and long waiting lists at the manufacturers. Then one would be forced to buy old tomato and orange boxes, which usually valueless, were suddenly in demand at a high price.

Using as many boxes as we did I decided to make our own. I imported the pine wood from Portugal, the main source of supply, and bought two heavy stapling machines. We had a splendid New Zealander and his girlfriend. They spent three months of the winter making boxes and when they went we put two of our own women on to the job. One of them, Mrs. Voakes, came up to the house saying her hand was aching. There was nothing to be seen but two small punctures. An idea occurred to Paula.

"Did you get hit by a staple?"

"Well I did check the machine against the palm of my hand."

Mrs. Voakes, driven by my son Richard who had passed his test the day before, was dispatched to hospital with a note from Paula saying that the hand must be

X-rayed. There deep among the bones, nerves and blood vessels of her hand was the heavy staple. It had to be extracted by a delicate operation. Mrs. Voakes never complained.

★ ★ ★

For some years I represented Sussex, Hampshire and Dorset on the National Farmers Union Apple Committee. While there I saw many statistics and it became clear that the only part of Europe that was not over producing apples was Ireland. When, in my apple selling trips to the north, I passed miles of small houses, I felt that England was in for a complete financial collapse. If that came, who would feed the ten million jobless from those houses? I would look for a farm in Ireland, which is under-populated and capable of being self sufficient.

The Ministry of Agriculture in London wrote to the Ministry of Agriculture in Dublin and off Paula and I went. On getting off the plane we were astonished to be met by the Ministry as honoured guests. They had worked out a programme for us and allocated someone to drive us round the country in a government car.

We came to the first fruit farm and looked at in horror. It was run down and derelict. The second and the third farms were just the same — they were a mess. As we worked down the coast towards Cork we did not see a farm on which apples were properly grown. It was not until the second day that I realised why they were treating me with such respect. London had given Dublin my production figures which at that time were one thousand tons of dessert apples. This, which was off one hundred acres, was equivalent to one third of the total production of Eire which came off several thousand acres. They thought they were dealing with one of the top English growers. I did not disillusion them.

At Waterford the Ministry had set up a meeting with the local growers. There were free sandwiches and whisky, and as the Irish are sociable, many growers had turned up. The official had set up soil maps of the county and indicated on it the areas where they recommended that I should start growing.

There were free sandwiches and whisky

"Do any of you know," he asked after discussing soils "whether there is any land available in the areas mentioned? Several of you here tonight have large farms, and perhaps you might be willing to sell some acres to help Mr Atkins start up. The Ministry feel it would be helpful to the fruit industry".

A senior farmer spoke up.

"I think it's very likely indeed that Mr Atkins will be able to buy just the land he wants. I remember well a farm which would have done him excellently. It sold only six years ago. At any time within the next ten years I am sure another suitable farm will become available; we will keep our eyes open". Others followed in the same vein.

They were only there for the party and the chat. Not one of them had the slightest intention of selling me any land whatsoever. Land hunger runs deep as blood in Irish veins.

It was a lucky escape because if we had bought land in Ireland we would have run up against their ingrained distrust of the English and that Irish attitude which is to promise everything and to do nothing.

We continued our enjoyable tour around those hospitable and dreadful farms. They were riddled with every possible disease but particularly with scab and canker. The trees, with their ties cutting deep into the bark and attached to rotting stakes, were crying out for help, but the farmers had no eyes to see. Twenty five years later they are still not growing apples with any success.

Each camp had its own special flavour. On one occasion we had the son of an African chief who, when he went back to Africa, wrote to me: 'One sweet memory of England which will always stay with me is your dulcet voice calling "Nine o'clock, nine o'clock. Out you come, or you'll be late!" He was quite serious about the 'sweet memory' and later sent me other members of his tribe for our camp.

Early on we had given up the idea of trying to get people up early. It is a long day doing physical work from nine to half past five. A late start enables one to organise the day and get the boxes out. By the time the pickers start the cold autumn dew is off the apples.

In the early days we felt ourselves responsible for the morals in the camp. We used to watch that in the morning they came out of the right caravan, the girls out of the girls' caravans and the men out of the mens' caravans. When I wanted somebody out early I would go along to their caravan and sometimes find that they were not there. We had one very pretty freckled girl, charming to look at, who I wanted out early one day to help. I went to her caravan and she wasn't there. I knew which caravan she would be in and I knocked at the door. I called

"Janet, we need you in the packing shed now".

She came out looking very sheepish.

"I was only cuddling, Mr Atkins, you must believe me, I was only cuddling".

At the final drinks party she came up to me.

"I would hate it if you thought the worse of me. I am a good girl, I really am". I believed her, she looked innocence itself.

It is an example of the change that has come across the country in the last twenty years that she should have been so defensive.

Two years later Janet Gay became the Milk Girl and pictures of her were plastered all over London. That lovely freckled face with the turned up nose looked down from every hoarding.

When we did a short television show on the farm I asked her to open it.

"You would think," said the introducer, "that Janet Gay, the Milk Girl, gets her beauty from milk, but she tells me that it is from milk and apples and these apples come from Tullens Toat. Here she is now to show you the farm".

Later we would see her freckled face in any advertisement which needed an outdoor girl. She also opened the film 'Far from the Madding Crowd', standing in for Julie Christie and riding a grey horse into the distance.

At one camp we had two girls on holiday from the BBC. After a couple of days they approached me.

"We don't think some of the men are getting enough to eat."

"I'll always give an advance of pay the first week to buy food." I replied.

"No, it's not that, they get up too late to cook. Would you mind if we cooked porridge for everyone?"

"Not in the least, but will they pay for it?"

"Oh we won't charge, we'll enjoy doing it and we're very well paid at the BBC."

From then on they held porridge parties at eight o'clock every morning. Anyone who turned up with a plate would have it filled. I sampled it myself one morning and it was excellent.

Another girl, encouraged by their example, made large quantities of apple jelly and also gave it away. I am continually astonished at the generosity of the young. When do most of us lose it?

They held porridge parties at eight o'clock every morning

The feeding habits of each caravan varies from those who live on steak and wine and those who live on spaghetti, cheese and tea. The spaghetti and cheese campers are in the majority, as the cost of steak horrifies them. Many of them also resent the cost of cleaning materials. They take these for granted in their family homes. One even said to me: "Cleaning things should be provided by the state".

When we had a number of caravans we had a girl to do the shopping. As she was asked to run all sorts of odd errands she had to be good natured. She also had to be numerate because it is quite a problem sorting out the charges for so many caravans. Sometimes a girl could do it easily in a notebook but others had to keep the money for each caravan in jam jars. None were allowed to give credit. I had had enough of unpaid bills landing on me.

The milkman came every day and he too quickly learnt not to give credit. Some campers saved considerable amounts of money while others were always out of money by Thursday evening. I can't see how you can drink a hundred pounds worth of beer in a week, but some manage to do so, and then ask for an advance of pay.

Vegetarians are getting more frequent. They are normally conscientious workers but we are wary of vegans. Their energy tends to peter out. As they do not eat any milk, eggs or cheese they have to get all their energy from nuts. We have had two vegans; the first one turned up in a genuine old smock, goodness knows from where he got it. He did his very best but he could not keep up the pace of apple picking and had to go.

The second, a vegetarian, worked well for us throughout the summer. After about six months he came up to me very upset.

"My girl friend is in a terrible state. One of the men where she works has tried to rape her. Can I bring her here?"

"Are you going to get married?"

"Of course", he said quite horrified. "I wouldn't dream of ruining her reputation."

There is a charming old world flavour to some vegetarians which is not shared by farm workers. My dear Mrs. Mills said to me early on:

"Now don't you set yourself up to judge morals, Master David, as long as people work well their morals be their own affair."

John married and brought his vegan wife to live in a caravan. I, in those brief days of prosperity, created a job for her. Then he too turned vegan and from that moment got weaker and weaker. Whatever the reason, and he was teased unmercifully by the staff, he gradually lost weight and strength. We were all sorry to see him go.

The first one turned up in a genuine old smock

On one camp we had the son of an Air Marshal and the daughter of a Harley Street specialist. They became friends and it all seemed most suitable. He had brought a van down with him and I later learned that each night he used to pile this with pillows and blankets and the two of them would go down to the river for the night.

Last to know as always I remarked, when in the early morning they drove in past me, how nice it must be getting up at dawn to walk by the river. Her family had not warned me that the girl was unstable and had a tendency to fall passionately in love. She was warm hearted, and sweet and I grew quite fond of her. I was touched on the last day when she kissed me an affectionate goodbye on the lips.

At the end of the camp they left with our best wishes. That evening her father rang up to ask when his daughter was coming home. I told him that she had just left. The couple had in fact gone to spend the night at Brighton and when she arrived home the following day she was met by a furious father. Quite unfairly he considered that we were to blame. The girl became pregnant and her Harley Street father could not let her have an abortion, which in those days was illegal. The matter was complicated because she was in love with the boy but he had been quickly shipped overseas by his family.

The girl's father must have written to The Times complaining about our camp because the next year, when we tried to put in an advertisement, we had to produce evidence that we ran a bona fide apple picking camp. In those days the papers were extremely strict. Later I learned that everyone in the camp and everybody on the staff knew perfectly well what was happening; I was the only one who believed they were going down to the river each dawn to walk hand in hand in sweet innocence through the dew drenched grass.

The girl's father must have written to the Times

* * *

We normally have swallows and martins around our barns. The swallows meet on our roof at about three o'clock to chat over the days affairs. They all arrive and leave together.

The martins need mud for their nests and are choosey about its quality. A friend, seeing many martins and few nests around his house put down piles of mud for them but after inspection they would not use it. Then he put the mud in a gutter and soon the nests increased from twelve to over sixty.

It is an astonishment to many campers to see how much wildlife we have on the farm. Badgers, deer, foxes, rabbits, hedgehogs, squirrels, pheasants, and large numbers of small birds. We had a Turk working for us who was wide-eyed with wonder.

"I live on the sea shore in Turkey," he said, "where we have woods all around us. I hardly ever see any animal or bird at all. Here they are all around our caravan at night".

Later when we were sailing round the coast of Turkey I realised that over the centuries man there had wiped out every bird and mammal. All along that wooded coast there is nothing left except turtles and they too are now in great danger. Europe has kept most of its animals and animal habitats because land owners over the centuries have preserved them for hunting. This is not generally understood by townsfolk.

★ ★ ★

Drugs did not hit us for about the first ten years. Then one year I noticed a number of plants growing in one of the caravans.

"How charming," I said, "but they are all one sort, no variety".

"Oh I love plants," said the girl clasping her hands "and this one will have the most lovely flowers".

It turned out to be cannabis. Later I learnt that that particular couple were dealing extensively in drugs. Unknown to all of us a son of a local was operating a distribution service across Sussex.

At this camp we had a good-looking young man of about thirty. He was an army helicopter pilot on secondment to one of the Gulf States where he was actively engaged in dealing with guerrillas. He was on extended leave and while not actually hunting for a wife, was ready to get married if he found the right girl. In the camp was a charming Australian girl with delicate features and green eyes, who was on a year's trip round the world. It was a gentle courtship but in the end she gave up her world trip and they got engaged. They were married eight weeks after they left us and we got an invitation to their wedding in Hereford.

* * *

The beginning of each crop is bound to have its mishap. One year, the stream of cars up to the pack house suddenly ceased. An Australian girl driving out at the wrong time, had pranged a picker's car and blocked the drive. Twenty cars were piled up below the accident. To her fury we manhandled her car into the ditch and let the flow restart.

Another year a South African missed the train that we had arranged to meet.

When he arrived and telephoned I pulled our youngest son away from making beer to go to the station. He roared off in his Renault 5. I had to give the camp lecture and I waited some time but the new camper did not arrive.

Meanwhile, my other son John coming back from the village found the traffic banked up at our crossroad. Driving illegally along the verge to reach our turn-off he saw Christopher's car askew and badly crushed. Beside it was a damaged Audi. A policeman came across.

"What do you think you're doing bypassing the traffic like that?"

"That's my brother's car," said John, "Is he badly hurt?"

"God knows how, but he got out alright, he seems only badly shaken. There he is."

Christopher and the other couple were being helped into an ambulance. The lightness of Christopher's car had saved him. It had been hit on the side and pushed ten yards along the road. He had emerged from his bashed in wreck by the passenger door.

★ ★ ★

A crop for which we felt well prepared started at full pressure but quickly ran into trouble. The telephone went from Stile Place Farm. It was the charge hand working under Alfred.

"One of the pickers has fallen off her ladder. Her finger has been torn off when her ring caught in a wire. What shall I do?"

"Have her driven to hospital at once".

A knock at the front door.

"Mrs Smith has fallen off her ladder and broken a leg".

Paula went out, examined the picker and soon one of our sons was on the way to hospital with the patient.

The telephone went again, it was the charge hand.

"We have found that finger".

"Send it to hospital at once". Off went another car.

Unfortunately the picker had gone to St Richards in Chichester while the finger went to the hospital in Worthing. They were never reunited but the picker was very brave and never complained. She came back to pick for us the following year.

Another knock on the door.

"A camper has been run over by a tractor".

Paula examined him, he seemed all right but was badly bruised and needed an X-ray. Another car set off for the hospital, four were now out at one time.

This was our worst day ever but every evening at six o'clock members of the camp, if ill, come up and see Paula. It has been a great help that she is a doctor.

On one occasion an Australian girl got very bad asthma and nearly died. We had her into the house and Paula nursed her for a week. She was a pleasant girl and most grateful. She should never have come to the camp and ever afterwards we made it clear that no-one who wasn't fully fit for the rigours of an autumn camp should apply.

A Brazilian boy who got pneumonia was another problem. He had nowhere to go to convalesce. Now all campers must give us a UK address with which we can get in touch.

The crop which started with so many accidents was one of Alfred's last. When Stile Place cottages were built he had moved across. Mrs. Funnell was in heaven with the wood block floor, the Aga in the kitchen, and two lavatories. He was nearing sixty five and his family asked us to a surprise party at which I was to present him with an engraved silver tray. The day of his retirement passed without a word. Surprise parties can be a mistake, and Alfred, feeling very neglected, grudgingly went out next day for a drink with his son to find that the family had taken the village hall. The press were there and in due course a picture appeared captioned:

"Mr. Funnell presenting his oldest employee, Mr. Atkins, with a testimonial gift".

Mr. Funnell presenting his oldest employee Mr Atkins with a testimonial gift

I kept Funnell on, but after a year he had a stroke. I went up to see him and he sat there crying and holding my hand. The early days of conflict were lost in the long years of joint effort. He had done his best for us and we were grateful.

★ ★ ★

Victoria plums are self-fertile, that is they don't need a pollinator. They are best planted on St. Julian A root-stock. In 1976 we put in three acres at fourteen foot by twelve foot. Like cherry trees, plum trees are very vulnerable to bacterial canker, which gets into any wound. One should not prune them until May; then, when the sap is running strongly, cuts heal quickly. Even so one has to paint each cut immediately it is made.

Plums flower early and are easily wiped out by April frosts. We grow them seven feet high and only use them for 'pick your own'. They are very sensitive to a certain weedkiller (call it 'X').

I was driving up one day to a fruit conference with Derek Chance, an excellent grower but new to plums. On the way up he asked me if there was anything special about growing them.

"Weeds on plums should be dealt with by small doses of Gramoxone, never use 'X'."

"Oh dear," said Derek, "I put four pounds of 'X' per acre on them yesterday."

At the conference my remark was confirmed. "Plums," said the lecturer, "are easily killed by any dose of 'X' over one pound per acre".

Derek's plums all flourished, while some of mine died.

The agony of growing plums is their destruction by frost. Although our plantation is about one hundred feet above sea level they have now been hit three years running, in 1989, 1990 and 1991. Over in Herefordshire it's the same. A high in the Atlantic gets and stays in position to the West of Ireland, this brings a downward sweep of cold air from the Arctic across England. In April we have a glorious show of blossom; this may survive three nights of slight frost from that deadly north wind. Then nature turns the screw tighter, the temperature drops from a survival level of 28.5 degrees fahrenheit, when no blossoms are killed, down to 27 degrees and next morning every single blossom is dead. By midday one can see the moisture of the shattered blossoms leaking their life-blood away. There is nothing you can do then, you can but sit and try not to weep in the pale sunlight, as you see a whole year's work, a whole year's effort, extinguished in one hour by a savage thrust of nature.

Now there is a new threat to Victoria plums. The Spanish have renamed the Vitt plum Victoriana. It crops at the same time, is similar in colour, but is slightly longer in shape and is insipid. This year, 1991, three days into the Victoria season they flooded all our markets with Victoriana. The wholesale price dropped in one day from 45 pence per lb to 15 pence. Is that the end of the Victoria plum?

★ ★ ★

In the cottage opposite Alan and Margaret we had a stream of occupants.

There was the family with the buxom pretty wife who worked so hard for her special charity. She collected in the valley for some months until I checked up with the charity itself and found she had never been heard of. No wonder she was always so well turned out.

Then there was the woman with delusions of grandeur. We had the teak weather boarding on our house replaced after thirty years.

"I see that the new timber comes from my ranch in Canada," she remarked, "I would give it to you free if it wasn't for the solicitor in the family trust. I'm afraid I shall have to charge you."

"When were you in Canada Mrs. Jones?"

"I was on tour as an opera singer. Instead of bringing the money back here to be taxed I bought this ranch. You must come and stay with us when we next go out."

When they had moved on we had a nice woman who kept on falling in love and running away. Twice she returned to her husband and there were floods of tears and happy reconciliations.

When she left for good we were away, Margaret Smith saw her pile everything into the car and drive off. Ten minutes later she was back with a screech of brakes. She ran into the house, came out with the Kenwood food mixer, and was off again for good.

11

Decline of English Orchards

THE time of hope in an apple grower's life is April. After the long slog of pruning through the rain and snow of January and February and the frosts of March, life returns to the countryside. Spring always comes too early for us; when the snowdrops show and the daffodil leaves begin to push up out of the ground, pruning is never finished. Until it is dry enough for the tractors to pass through the orchards and mash the prunings, no sprayer can move across the fields. The flail masher gives me constant pleasure. There are seven trace elements in growing apples and these are now chopped up and returned to the soil. With the leaves also being taken in by the worms it is only the apples that take any nutrient from the orchards.

No longer do we spray the trees in

the depth of winter with tar oil, that tough clogging spray that killed all over-wintering eggs, not only of our enemies such as red spider and aphides, but also of the insects who fight on our side. Following a bad attack of spider in the autumn, their eggs would be so thick along the branches that the trees looked a reddish bronze. For the moment at least we have them under control by our best predator the Typh mite (Typhlodromus Pyri). One's fear, however, is that with a hot summer the spiders will breed so fast that the predators, sluggish with overeating, will be swamped. Each red spider can in one month have 160,000 offspring while a typh can only eat 20 a day. In hot weather we have had an orchard bronzing in a few days. Once the juice is sapped from a leaf it never recovers. The apples lack colour

while a typh can only eat 20 a day

and vitality and stop growing and on top of that next year's fruit buds are undernourished and poor.

It is in August to September that the bud finally makes up its mind as to whether next year it will be a fruit bud or only carry leaves. Even if it makes the decision to be a blossom bud it may still, if not treated right, be ghost bloom. This is a pale flower with no tinge of pink and incapable of bearing an apple. The sight of ghost bloom in an orchard is a warning of failure to come, because all the other blooms are likely to be weak. This type of bloom is only found in Cox; the Golden Delicious, the Lambourne and the James Grieve never have it.

With the pruning finished, the avenues mashed and clear of branches, one comes to the movement of the buds. Anxiously as the March days lengthen one watches the skies. Please let there be cloud at night and a south west wind. No lover looks at a girl more ardently than the fruit grower watches the weather.

"She offered him the solace of a mouth
Warm as the west wind, fragrant as the
south."

Slowly the buds open, the aphides (green or black fly) gather for their attack. They cluster at the edge of each bud waiting to get in to feed. In the late 1950s this was the only moment, two days at most, at which one could catch them, and one applied a contact spray. Now one can let them in, they start feeding, the buds cry out for help and gently as a caress of a hand on a child's hair, at five gallons of water and four fluid ounces of spray material to the acre, the droplets spread onto every bud. I've seen gardeners use as much chemical on a dozen rose trees as we use on an orchard.

Clear of the aphides the bud grows and strengthens, still the wind is in the west, April is half way through. Mouse ear is past and so is green cluster, and now comes pink bud and the tortrix caterpillars. One delays as long as possible to get them all hatched, but not a day too long. We used to use DDT, that vicious invention that world wide has wiped out so much wild life and is still being used by the World Health Organisation in the third world. Now we use a gentler spray which will spare all predator insects, but, because caterpillars eat leaves, will get them alone.

Still there is hope. Surely one can rely on seven hundred thirty pound boxes per acre, and surely, if the public is going to pay forty pence or more per pound, one should get ten pence a pound back to the orchards. That is the minimum we need to break even.

With the bloom out one is still watching the weather. The wind swings to the north west and then to the north and then settles in to that dread position, the east.

"When the wind be in the East it be no good for man or beast".

The ground dries up, the buds cease to grow, the leaves become pallid in the cold and we wait for the still clear night and the frost. Even against the east wind we can survive but not, oh not, against that light breeze from the north east. It rolls across from Norfolk, dropping all its moisture as it goes. Across England it comes until it reaches the Weald and here it gathers twenty miles of freezing air and piles it up against Toat hill. The frost savages the two small apple farms on the north slope, and then, if the wind is over two miles an hour, it drives the frost over our shelter belt onto our long southern slope. Here it runs down the hill and begins to fill the valley between us and the greensand ridge. The ridge is taller than our hill and slowly the frost backs up into our orchards.

The morning comes and reveals the hoar frost lying thick and white, not only in the valley, but right up along the hill, In six hours one will be able to tell by examining a selection of buds how much damage has been done. If the centre of a bud is brown, the bloom is dead.

If we have escaped the frost and while the bloom is still open, sure as debts and death, comes the blackthorn winter, How long will it last? One sad year (1974) every farm to the west of us flowered two days before the cold spell and every farm to the east of us two days later. All of them had an adequate crop; the blackthorn winter had caught only West Sussex where all the farms were devastated. In a cold spell nothing will pollinate. The male pollen tube grows so slowly down to the female ovary that it dies on its way and never gets there.

If one comes through this then, at petal fall, the sawfly attacks. This has been much less rampant recently and, because of the danger to the bees, we do not spray but let it do its worst.

Now it is mid May and every day that passes the pollinated apples strengthen their fragile hold on life. Growers develop "flicking finger". The king apple, that misshapen centre apple with the long throat, is better gone, but one needs two out of the five blossoms to hold. The good apples are now growing at half a millimetre diameter a day. They develop a mauve colour and a certain firmness. The others hesitate. Will they cling? Soon some shrivel and brush off to the touch of a finger while the others plump up.

If four apples out of each truss cling one faces the next burden; these four have ideally to be reduced to two. If they are not they won't make the size and the bud, exhausted by it's burden, will not have the energy to make another fruit bud for next year. That is what happens in gardens where trees frequently crop in alternate years.

When the apple is twelve millimetres in diameter it is probably safe from frost. A warm June is vital to Cox as only in that month are the cells laid down; a cold June will give fewer cells and the apples will be small. Now it is the middle of June and the decision to thin or not to thin has got to be made. If one decides to thin one will need twelve extra women to work over every branch on the farm. By the end of June it is a matter of warmth and water and hope. The June drop which comes in early July is unpredictable. Towards the end of June the trees decide which apples to throw and which to keep. It varies between a drop of 15 per cent up to as much as 70 per cent. Annoyingly the higher figure normally applies to fast growing trees which need to be tamed by a heavy crop. Like a headstrong horse the trees do the reverse of what you want. Horizontal branches tend to bear apples and upright branches to grow and the tree is always trying to grow taller.

Now the remaining perils are hail and gales. In August gales up to force eight or even nine can be weathered, but force ten jerks the branches and the apples fall. When Edward Heath's yacht went down in the Solent it was in a force ten gale and when I went out next day some twenty or thirty thousand pounds worth of apples lay on the ground. They were too immature to pick up. They had no value.

★ ★ ★

1978

Each camp tends to be dominated by one or two people. If one puts twenty hens in a yard or twenty cows in a field, within a week each one will know its place in the pecking order. It's much the same in caravan camps. It is a basic fact of life, and makes nonsense of the theory of the equality of human beings who are only a type of animal.

In 1978 Jock, a kilted Scot of about twenty five, well educated, bearded and strong, quickly became dominant. He looked like Rasputin. He drank a bottle of whisky a day and was understood to be connected with the Black Watch. He was very hard working and even when drunk managed to fulfil his difficult job in the grading shed. Around the area in which he worked he put up signs in schoolboy Latin, some being personal remarks about the girls. They were relatively inoffensive. One was, "Joan has the most beautiful breasts", another "noli illegitimus carborundum", translates to "Don't let the bastard wear you down". Whether it referred to me or to Alan I never knew.

Jock was extremely dirty and was rumoured never to wash his clothes, but to rewear them after giving them a week's rest. Some girls, however, found him very attractive. As the camp thinned out no man would share a caravan with him and this left him the privacy of an empty caravan for his pleasures.

As he continued to dominate the camp the other men seemed to get younger and less effective. Only a few of the more discerning girls stood apart.

He regularly ran out of money before payday on Saturday and on Friday night, having failed to borrow from me, would run up bills in the pub; these he could be relied upon to repay. He was a good driver and, having assured me he had a clean licence, I detailed him to do most of the driving at night. It was the days before the campaign on drinking and driving, and certainly throughout that long autumn, however drunk he was he never scratched the van.

The dispatch bay requires somebody capable of lifting forty-pound boxes five feet high for hour after hour, and this he was able to do. When therefore it was time for half of the camp to go, I asked him to stay on. It was not until the farewell drinks party that I learnt that those girls that he had not been able to obtain he disconcerted by flashing; he was rumoured to be unusually well-endowed.

His attitude to me was subtle in that, without apparently currying favour, he nevertheless managed to do so. On my birthday he led up a party to sing happy birthday, and brought up a present of a bottle of whisky for him and me to share.

"Come on you frosty-faced bastard", he said, "I've never seen you drunk yet".

"Timeo Danaos et dona ferentes" (I fear campers who bring me gifts), I replied from my small stock of Latin, but it was my birthday and he drank me silly. Paula thoroughly distrusted him and thought he was taking me for a ride. How right she was.

This was one of our most memorable camps. In it there was a South African, who not for any high motive, had defaulted from his military service in his country. He always had an eye out for personal gain, and having learnt that there was a black market for passports in Earls Court, he went up and sold his. This was in the days before South African passports became unwanted.

He then reported to me that he had had his passport stolen and I, as a county councillor, endorsed his application for a fresh one. Jock heard of this and told me what had happened. When the new passport arrived I signed for it and posted it straight back to the Embassy with a covering note to say that the applicant had now found his passport. The man left in a huff; I wonder how he managed.

When the camp work was finally finished and Jock was paid off, he and one of the prettiest girls disappeared with my van. I reported the theft to the police and I now began to get some feedback on Jock's real past; instead of being the son of an officer in the Black Watch as he had implied he turned out to be the son of a gamekeeper on a big estate. Where he had got his impeccable English I do not know.

After the two had been gone for some weeks I received a letter from the Dorchester Hotel, saying that Jock had applied for a job as a doorkeeper and had given my name as a reference. I informed the police who found Jock already working at the hotel, recovered the van, and arrested him.

They prosecuted him for the theft of the van and in the course of this his driving licence was suspended for three years. When the sentence was passed the police discovered that, although he had been driving for several years, he had never had a licence. Poor Jock, he must be dead by now. No one can drink several bottles of whisky a week and still be going strong. May he rest in peace, he certainly enlivened life wherever he was and that year is remembered on the farm as "Jock's year".

★ ★ ★

When I came into farming, like all business men, I thought it would be a piece of cake. I would be competing against slower witted growers.

It did not take me long to realise that English farmers are not merely efficient, they are far more efficient than most businessmen. Paradoxically that is their great weakness. The production of food in England per acre is higher than in Europe or America. We top Europe both in production per man and production per acre. America beats us in production per man, but this is largely due to their vast prairie type corn growing. Our production per acre is far higher than theirs.

The average farmer in the Northern hemisphere spends less than ten per cent of his time and money on administration. This low figure cannot be equalled by most businesses and financial institutions. The result of this efficiency is that food is so plentiful that the producer does not receive a reasonable share of the sale price. With milk, the farmer now gets 9p out of a sale price of 34p.

When a successful businessman goes into fruit growing one is almost certain he will fail. The last big failure was a vegetable wholesaler who had run a public company. It took him eight years to realise that nature does not grow to order, and he sold out his large acreage of apples and lettuce at a very considerable loss. Growers are frequently urged to computerise their farms, so that they can know the cost of everything they do. If something needs doing and there's no alternative, there's no point in knowing the cost. Only if knowledge would help in making a decision do you need records. An apple grower, apart from the ordinary financial results, needs one main bit of information; the yearly production rate of each orchard is absolutely vital. This is not all that easy to get. With four temporary tractor drivers hauling in the trailers or the bins, it is very easy for them to forget to book the apples against the correct orchard and this has to be watched closely.

★ ★ ★

The deer on our farm eat the young trees and are far more of a nuisance than foxes. Early on we tried to shoot them ourselves. One evening in the gloaming I stood among the young oak trees where I thought they had bedded down for the day. One of my staff was concealed at the expected exit point. As the sun went down there was nothing to be seen and then like apparitions, within 20 yards of me, three deer silently stood up. I moved slightly and they ran straight in the direction we had planned. One shot and the buck was dead.

I felt no pleasure as I knew that I had broken up a family. From that day I have opted out of deer shooting and handed it over to an expert. Every year he culls three deer and the death and the gutting keep the orchards clear for some

The way to protect young trees is to hang lion's dung from the branches.

months. The way to protect young trees and roses from deer attacks is, so it is said, to hang human hair or lions dung in bags on the branches. It would be an awful lot of work.

The poaching of deer and pheasants is a problem. In the early dawn, our authorised shooter saw two men with guns standing near the reservoir. He walked quietly up behind them and when he was three yards away cocked his gun. They turned, looked at his gun and ran as fast as they could.

Four o'clock one morning our friendly ivory coloured retriever, Riski, started making a great fuss, I went down and let him out. When Paula went down at half past seven he was lying on the doorstep shocked and bleeding badly. Someone had cut off half his ear. It was a clean cut done with a knife. We think Riski, with his usual good temper, had bounded down to say hello to a poacher who was lying in wait for the deer. Dogs tend to be noisy and to get Riski to leave him alone I think the poacher took out his knife and, while patting him, cut off a slice of his ear. Riski lost a great deal of blood but the real shock was to his belief that all men were his dear friends.

Now that we shoot pheasants regularly on the farm we put up a great many deer. It is illegal to shoot them with a twelve bore so we let them go past. I have been surprised to see how, when frightened, they run full pelt into fences. Recently a poor foal broke her neck in front of me. The heartless mother jumped the fence and went on without a backward glance.

We never used to encourage shooting, but with the drop in income we have been forced into diversification (that popular word). The first year we put down one hundred pheasants and did not shoot one. The local poachers saw to that. We changed our keeper and since then have gradually increased the number of birds we put down to 900 of which we normally shoot some 350. The rest wander away or live to breed.

Pheasants are most intriguing. Brought in and released into a pen in July, for four weeks they stay protected, but as soon as they are big enough they are allowed free and start to wander, returning only at night.

At first they go out in groups of the same sex. Hen birds and cock birds keep on their own, eyeing each other from a distance, and giggling and whispering to each other about the other groups. The cocks are braver than the hens and by early September have found their way all over the farm. Sometimes in the early morning we will find eight or ten cocks sitting on our garden wall. The hens are never so cheeky. All of them, however, grow and get braver day by day until the shooting season starts. We rarely shoot in October and this lets them get up their strength and confidence.

How do they know that shooting is starting? Driving to a shoot in Goodwood one day, I passed fifty pheasants sitting on an oak fence near a wood. They watched me go by. Half an hour later we drove the same wood and hardly a pheasant came out. They know instinctively about shooting and I believe they can read our minds from a distance. Dogs also understand about

Other people's dogs aren't so well trained

the shooting season. Until there is a shoot Riski will walk within six feet of a pheasant and leave it alone and the pheasant will face him unafraid. Other people's dogs aren't so well trained!

Out of fifty pheasants in a wood probably only twenty will fly. The others hide in holes or undergrowth or run sideways. As the season progresses the more stupid pheasants get shot and the clever ones learn to fly low along the hedges. On the very day that the season is over the remaining pheasants emerge and strut around. They know that they are safe. How do they know that?

In the summer they become most aggressive.

"We can't prune the loganberries," said two girls, "a pheasant keeps on attacking us. He flies at our faces and pecks".

Richard went down and as he worked beside them a pheasant came up behind and pecked at his fingers. He continued to prune and the pheasant flew at his face and tried to rake it with his spurs. It was only when he hit it with a stick that it backed off.

All spring and summer we have resident pheasants who, wise in the ways of men and foxes, take up their chosen positions. Their timorous hens join them but keep low and out of sight. There is certainly no equality of sexes in the pheasant world. This year our own house pheasant, when we did not put out food, marched past our dog into the dining room, and snatched bread from the table.

When a hen pheasant sits on eggs it closes its feathers so tightly that no dog or fox can scent her. As she is almost invisible she can only be found by chance.

Because of danger, on our shoot we shoot no foxes or rabbits; because of sentiment we shoot no partridges, duck or woodcock all of which pair for life. It is a pheasant-only shoot and we do not grudge the sixty per cent who fly or run sideways to live another day. If there were no shoots there would be no pheasants. I think pheasants would prefer to live their short but enjoyable lives than never be hatched.

★ ★ ★

Because hills tend to be conical there is less land high up than there is low down, The low fields are subject to frost and are used for grazing. Grazing only costs £30 per acre in Sussex, but £80 per acre in Gloucestershire and elsewhere. So much land in Sussex is owned by rich men who earn their income elsewhere that it does not matter to them what they get for their fields.

One does not let grazing, one sells the grass for a maximum of 364 days. Only by this means can one stop the occupier obtaining a right to keep the land for his lifetime. Cows are the most aggressive of the grazing animals. They see a fence and say to themselves:

"Let's give it a little push here and a little push there, and we'll soon get it down".

If they can't knock it down some of them will wriggle under, I could hardly believe my eyes when I saw a heifer lie down beside a barbed wire fence, ease herself below the lower strand and wriggle under. Cows do not always dung in the same place, so the fields do not deteriorate.

Horses take a look at a fence and say to themselves.

"That's a fence, we had better stay this side of it".

As however they always dung in the same area they tend to ruin fields. This dunging area, where they won't graze, soon becomes an overgrown mess unless one spreads the dung frequently with a harrow. Even then they won't go back to their dunging area and one needs to bring in sheep or cattle to clear the field up.

Sheep also test the defences and break

I do hate them sheep
They be unaccountable
cackhanded

through if possible. If while doing so they can fall upside down in a shallow ditch, they will do so and then lie there passively until they die.

"I do hate them sheep," said Alfred, "They be unaccountable cackhanded (clumsy)".

Fruit growers, in order to reduce spraying against caterpillar and codlin, use pheromone traps. These give off the mating smells of female moths. We use three types; for codling moth and for two species of tortrix caterpillar. Only when one has caught sufficient of the male insects, which in the case of the codling moth is five for two weeks running, or of tortrix caterpillar which is thirty in one week, does one spray. The objective is to target that moth only and not to hurt any others. This cuts sprays down to a maximum of three a year at low concentrations because one knows the moths are there and vulnerable.

Early in the 1960s, in order to reduce sprays, I tacked corrugated cardboard rings around the trees. The female codling grub climbed up from the soil and to pupate took up its quarters in the folds of the cardboard. They were moving in so quickly that the bluetits, within the week, had torn all the cardboard to tatters and had cleared the grubs. It was very rewarding, but when wages rose, was too labour intensive.

Perhaps, if one put out enough pheromone traps one could trap most of the male moths and then one would not need to spray at all.

My son Richard when working in South Africa was horrified to find that there they sprayed up to five times for codling and I believe they do the same in America.

For red spider control in strawberries we can now get phytoseilus mites, which we scatter along the rows. They are like tigers in a jungle and hunt down the strawberry red spider, which oddly enough is green, with speed and ferocity. With six types of anthocorid, a relation to the human bed bug, also rampaging around after aphides we have come a long way from relying only on sprays.

Throughout horticulture the effort to cut out chemicals has had great success. White fly is now destroyed by parasitic wasps, leaf miner by another parasite, thrips on capsicum and on cucumber by predatory mites and, of course the great success, the red spider is eaten up by typh mites which can destroy up to twenty young spiders in a day, and can travel quite long distances to do so.

I'm not so happy about the research on introducing viruses and bacteria into insects. I think it might backfire on the world. By all means have pests eaten by other insects, but to infect them with diseases seems dangerous and unfair.

There is nothing new under the sun. The Chinese in 300 AD used to protect their citrus trees from caterpillars by the use of predatory ants. In 2,500 BC the Sumerians in Iraq were spraying sulphur on fruit and in 1,200 BC the Chinese were using insecticides.

★ ★ ★

The downfall of English Apple growing has crept up on us slowly. There have been four long term causes. The rise in wages was overdue, but soon the agricultural worker's rate passed that for shop assistants, hotel workers, and most factory workers. Three hundred boxes of apples used to pay a years wages, now it is two thousand boxes. This would not have mattered if the rise in apple prices had even begun to keep pace. A good man in 1953 was paid £6.00 per week, Now he is paid about £9,000 a year, which with the farm's share of national insurance comes to £10,000. Of this the Government through tax and national insurance takes nearly 30%. Thus the rise in wages, well earned, has amounted to 3000% while the rise in prices has only been one fifth of that. To run this small farm in 1990 cost us £3,000 per week — £600 per working day. £150,000 to break even is an awful lot of money to get out of apples. Of this sum, directly and indirectly, I believe over £50,000 goes to the Government.

The planting of so many apples in France was a disaster for us. Golden Delicious yield three times as much per acre as Cox. Add to that the French government gives their growers low interest rates. Furthermore it does not police the taking of "intervention" on apples. This is a subsidy of two pence per pound given to destroy some apples, but in France the subsidy is taken and then the same apples are sold on illegally. No, I can't prove the statement but I believe it to be true.

Through amalgamations and take overs only six supermarket chains are now left, and their buyers have tremendous bargaining power. Some pay lip service to helping the English grower, but when the chips are down they rarely do so. They use their power ruthlessly. For example if they have over-ordered they refuse good apples on the grounds of quality, and, as they have very little storage space, they insist that apples are delivered every day to every branch. To cope with this I now deliver my apples to a main cooperative, Home Grown Fruits, which collects most of the apples from Kent and Sussex in a vast aerodrome hangar and then from there plans journeys the same night for delivery nationwide. The cost of transport is heavy. Supermarket staff have little idea of how to handle apples and the Cox, being particularly easy to bruise, often ends up battered and ugly, very different from the lovely fruit that was originally packed. It is quite heartbreaking.

Size is the final nail in our coffin. While Cox grows naturally to a diameter of sixty millimetres (two and a quarter inches), Golden Delicious and American apples grow to about seventy millimetres (two and three quarter inches). The supermarket likes big apples, and although the public say they prefer the smaller ones, I have watched too many people in my apple shop choose the larger size to believe that any other than the really discerning go for the smaller size. A Cox, however small, has the true Cox flavour and as small ones are cheap they are a good buy.

When I used to open the Worcester season in London I had a regular visit from a fruiterer who sold in the Kings Road. Stout, red-faced, short of breath, down he would come:

"I must see the start of the English apple season, Mr. Atkins. Your apples are moreish."

"What do you mean, moorish?" I asked.

"My customers put their teeth into them and always come back for more."

In those days everything I picked each day was graded the same afternoon, reached Covent Garden by five a.m. next morning, was sold by six a.m. and out in the shops the same day. On Friday we never picked because of the lack of sales on Saturday. We left them on the trees to grow over the weekend.

One day I dropped in on Harrods and asked to see the food buyer.

"My name is Atkins," I started.

"Tullens Toat, Pulborough," he replied, "we always buy your apples."

Those days have gone, and now it takes up to a week to get apples from the tree into a supermarket and sold.

★ ★ ★

I have written little about the recent years as I have not yet got them in perspective. In 1986 the apple industry took a real turn for the worse. A warm spring and cold summer meant that there was an abundant crop of Cox apples of under

376

Soon like cuckoos in July
we may have to give up and go

sixty five millimetre. All over England apples that year lacked the fine Cox flavour. They were not "moreish". The price collapsed and more than ninety per cent of the apple growers in England made a serious loss. Most of the Kent farmers paid off their overdrafts by selling off farm cottages.

I wrote to my eldest son in South Africa saying that the farm had no future. When he came back he went into his old profession as a chartered surveyor.

My wife and her dog.

We have tottered on earning less than 1% on capital. A young man could not now go into apple growing and succeed. We are down from three thousand growers in 1954 to eight hundred now and those who have survived mostly have farm shops or other income. It will be sad if the apple farms of England are finally forced out of business. Not only are they beautiful in themselves, but they supply the best flavoured fruit in the world, a fruit which is vital to health. Soon, like cuckoos in July, we apple growers may have to give up, defeated by the climate.

Next time you buy Coxes, think for a moment of the intricate work by the trees, the insects and the people which has gone into their production.

THE TWILIGHT MAN
Frank Gruber

Jim Rand lives alone in the California desert awaiting death. Into his hermit existence comes a teenage girl who blows both his past and his brief future wide open.

DOG IN THE DARK
Gerald Hammond

Jim Cunningham breeds and trains gun dogs, and his antagonism towards the devotees of show spaniels earns him many enemies. So when one of them is found murdered, the police are on his doorstep within hours.

THE RED KNIGHT
Geoffrey Moxon

When he finds himself a pawn on the chessboard of international espionage with his family in constant danger, Guy Trent becomes embroiled in moves and countermoves which may mean life or death for Western scientists.

THE WILDERNESS WALK
Sheila Bishop

Stifling unpleasant memories of a misbegotten romance in Cleave with Lord Francis Aubrey, Lavinia goes on holiday there with her sister. The two women are thrust into a romantic intrigue involving none other than Lord Francis.

THE RELUCTANT GUEST
Rosalind Brett

Ann Calvert went to spend a month on a South African farm with Theo Borland and his sister. They both proved to be different from her first idea of them, and there was Storr Peterson — the most disturbing man she had ever met.

ONE ENCHANTED SUMMER
Anne Tedlock Brooks

A tale of mystery and romance and a girl who found both during one enchanted summer.

TIGER TIGER
Frank Ryan

A young man involved in drugs is found murdered. This is the first event which will draw Detective Inspector Sandy Woodings into a whirlpool of murder and deceit.

CAROLINE MINUSCULE
Andrew Taylor

Caroline Minuscule, a medieval script, is the first clue to the whereabouts of a cache of diamonds. The search becomes a deadly kind of fairy story in which several murders have an other-worldly quality.

LONG CHAIN OF DEATH
Sarah Wolf

During the Second World War four American teenagers from the same town join the Army together. Forty-two years later, the son of one of the soldiers realises that someone is systematically wiping out the families of the four men.

MORNING IS BREAKING
Lesley Denny

The growing frenzy of war catapults Diane Clements into a clandestine marriage and separation with a German refugee.

LAST BUS TO WOODSTOCK
Colin Dexter

A girl's body is discovered huddled in the courtyard of a Woodstock pub, and Detective Chief Inspector Morse and Sergeant Lewis are hunting a rapist and a murderer.

THE STUBBORN TIDE
Anne Durham

Everyone advised Carol not to grieve so excessively over her cousin's death. She might have followed their advice if the man she loved thought that way about her, but another girl came first in his affections.

CLOUD OVER MALVERTON
Nancy Buckingham

Dulcie soon realises that something is seriously wrong at Malverton, and when violence strikes she is horrified to find herself under suspicion of murder.

AFTER THOUGHTS
Max Bygraves

The Cockney entertainer tells stories of his East End childhood, of his RAF days, and his post-war showbusiness successes and friendships with fellow comedians.

MOONLIGHT
AND MARCH ROSES
D. Y. Cameron

Lynn's search to trace a missing girl takes her to Spain, where she meets Clive Hendon. While untangling the situation, she untangles her emotions and decides on her own future.

NURSE ALICE IN LOVE
Theresa Charles

Accepting the post of nurse to little Fernie Sherrod, Alice Everton could not guess at the romance, suspense and danger which lay ahead at the Sherrod's isolated estate.

POIROT INVESTIGATES
Agatha Christie

Two things bind these eleven stories together — the brilliance and uncanny skill of the diminutive Belgian detective, and the stupidity of his Watson-like partner, Captain Hastings.

LET LOOSE THE TIGERS
Josephine Cox

Queenie promised to find the long-lost son of the frail, elderly murderess, Hannah Jason. But her enquiries threatened to unlock the cage where crucial secrets had long been held captive.

BUTTERFLY MONTANE
Dorothy Cork

Parma had come to New Guinea to marry Alec Rivers, but she found him completely disinterested and that overbearing Pierce Adams getting entirely the wrong idea about her.

HONOURABLE FRIENDS
Janet Daley

Priscilla Burford is happily married when she meets Junior Environment Minister Alistair Thurston. Inevitably, sexual obsession and political necessity collide.

WANDERING MINSTRELS
Mary Delorme

Stella Wade's career as a concert pianist might have been ruined by the rudeness of a famous conductor, so it seemed to her agent and benefactor. Even Sir Nicholas fails to see the possibilities when John Tallis falls deeply in love with Stella.

THE LISTERDALE MYSTERY
Agatha Christie

Twelve short stories ranging from the light-hearted to the macabre, diverse mysteries ingeniously and plausibly contrived and convincingly unravelled.

TO BE LOVED
Lynne Collins

Andrew married the woman he had always loved despite the knowledge that Sarah married him for reasons of her own. So much heartache could have been avoided if only he had known how vital it was to be loved.

ACCUSED NURSE
Jane Converse

Paula found herself accused of a crime which could cost her her job, her nurse's reputation, and even the man she loved, unless the truth came to light.